# AND THEY CALL THEM GAMES

# AND THEY CALL THEM GAMES

## AN INSIDE VIEW OF THE
## 1996 OLYMPICS

C. Richard Yarbrough

MERCER UNIVERSITY PRESS
2000

ISBN 0-86554-706-8
MUP/H524

First Edition.

The author and publisher are grateful to the Watson Brown Foundation for a generous subvention supporting the publication of this book.

∞The paper used in this publication meets the minimum requirements of American National Standard for Information Sciences — Permanence of Paper for Printed Library Materials, ANSI Z39.48-1984.

*Library of Congress Cataloging-in-Publication Data*

Yarbrough, C. Richard.
And they call them games: an inside view of the 1996 Olympics / C. Richard Yarbrough. — 1st ed.
p. cm.
Includes index.
ISBN 0-86554-706-8 (alk. paper)
1. Olympic Games (26th: 1996: Atlanta, Ga.) I. Title.

GV722 1996. Y37 2000
796.48 — dc21                                              00-056878

# TABLE OF CONTENTS

*For Jane, my enduring soul mate and wise counselor. For Ken and Jackie, Maribeth and Ted, who gave me the greatest gift imaginable: Zachary, Brian, Nicholas and Thomas. And for JoAnne Kessler, my friend.*

# ACKNOWLEDGMENTS

NO BOOK EVER WENDS THE DIFFICULT PATH FROM IDEA TO PRINT WITHOUT A lot of people along the way to cajole, correct, criticize, and cheer. This epistle is no exception. It started with long-time political observer, Bill Shipp convincing me to dust off my records and tell people what really happened in Atlanta, both the good and the bad. For many years, he and I were the "cobra and the mongoose" of media relations as he plied his trade for the Atlanta newspapers and I defended the moat at the telephone company. Many people find it incredulous that we are now working together. We find it amusing.

Nicholas Wolaver, an Olympic enthusiast and rising public relations star, provided me background material and helpful hints. Both of which were invaluable.

I had only nine weeks to get my thoughts on paper. As always, JoAnne Kessler rescued me. This Superwoman took my taped ramblings and transcribed them to paper. The task was made even more difficult in that I dictated in the car with horns blowing, telephones ringing, me forgetting where I was when I turned the tape back on and lots of whining, angst and anger as I described each day's activities. Nonetheless, she gave me back some 1,200 pages, double-spaced and tabbed. She is unbelievable.

My agent and chief proof reader, Jane Yarbrough, saw every page off the printer, edited the typos and sent me back to clear up the confusing sentences and to get rid of the bad ones. Once by her eagle eye, the words received more polish by Marc Jolley, Mercer Press assistant publisher, who also counseled temperance when I got a little too blunt. What he took out I have saved and will sneak them in my columns from time to time. They were too good to waste. Photographs were mostly a family affair. Knowing I was only going to do this once, I took a lot of pictures. Jane also took quite a few. Maribeth Yarbrough Wansley, who could be a professional photographer, if she wasn't so busy raising a husband, two sons, two dogs and saving Planet Earth as an environmentalist, loaned me some of hers. They are excellent. I also thank Ross Henderson for his counsel on photographs as well as the photo of me on the cover.

Rick O'Quinn, at the University of Georgia gave me permission to use the beautiful sunset over Sanford Stadium and the ever-efficient Ann

Bovaird of the White House press office okayed the picture of President Clinton handing the torch to Carla McGhee at the White House.

There are a lot of factoids in the Olympic Games and I have shared those numbers with some expert fact checkers. They include my boss, Billy Payne, who has read the manuscript and given me his thoughts. I also checked facts and figures with A. D. Frazier, ACOG's chief operating officer, Pat Glisson, chief financial officer, and Rod Knowles, our technology managing director. How I got to ACOG to work on the Centennial Games and then write about them was as a result of a lot of people who came along in my life as I needed them: My mom and dad, Bessie Mae and Earl Yarbrough, who gave me equal parts of drive and integrity; my brother, Bob, who was my role model; Dr. Raymond Cook, who saved my college career at Georgia State, and Dean John Drewry, who honed it at UGA. Then there were the mentors: the late Jasper Dorsey, my boss at Southern Bell and one of the most important figures in my life. I'm still living in his shadow. Wallace Bunn, the first chairman of BellSouth, who showed me that one could be successful in the corporate world and be a real gentleman at the same time, and John Clendenin, who taught me that glibness and guts aren't enough. You have to know your facts. Bob Holder became not only my friend but my most important and most patient counselor. Finally, there are Harold Burson and John Budd, two great practitioners in New York who have forgotten more public relations than I will ever hope to know.

Certainly, no book would have been written if it had not been for the 100,000 men and women who put on the 1996 Centennial Olympic Games. I acknowledge them all proudly.

DY

# PROLOGUE

When I joined the Atlanta Committee for the Olympic Games in January 1993, I realized I would be a part of history. Atlanta was going to host the most significant event in its history (if you don't count William Tecumseh Sherman's stroll through town 132 years earlier), and I was going to have a major role to play in it. The Centennial Olympic Games were coming to Atlanta in 1996.

Like so many other Atlantans, I was pleased but not surprised that our city had been chosen to host the world. After all, I told myself, we are Atlanta. These kinds of miracles happen here. Little did I know at the time how long and how hard Billy Payne and a number of other volunteers had worked to win the Olympic Games for the city. The miracle wasn't that Atlanta won; it was that Payne had the stamina, confidence, and creativity to pull it off. He would need large measures of all three before the Games were over.

At the time the Games were awarded to Atlanta, I never imagined I would be a part of the planning committee. I had a great job as vice president of BellSouth, one of the "Baby Bells" that had been created a few years earlier with the breakup of the Bell System. Through force of persuasion, personality, and hard work, I had managed at BellSouth to give the discipline of public relations something it lacked in many companies—respect. My CEO, John Clendenin, had given me ample opportunity to practice my craft at a senior level and to have some influence in the decisions of the corporation. Just as attorneys provide legal counsel, my job was to provide the corporation external counsel.

I was the envy of many of my colleagues around the country who considered my situation near unique. Many public relations practitioners have little impact on how their organizations do business. They aren't at the table helping make the decisions. They merely produce somebody else's. I was lucky and I knew it.

Not that Clendenin was easy to deal with. He wasn't. Like most chief executive officers, he was bright, opinionated, and could be downright intimidating if he knew something that he thought he was paying you to know. He allowed me to argue with him when I felt strongly about an issue. But it was important that I was right in my arguments. He wouldn't accept my advice just because I thought it was good; he had to be convinced, as well. The result would be an endless string of tough questions until he decided my counsel was correct.

But it meant that top management would give serious consideration to the impact of the external environment. It was my job to be sure they always did.

That reputation for strong external advocacy caught the attention of Bob Holder, co-chairman of the board of the Atlanta Committee and a friend of Clendenin's. He thought that I could be helpful in getting the committee through the formidable hurdles it faced in the external environment. Clearly, the euphoria was over in Atlanta and the critics, special interest groups, and doubters were in full force.

Leaving BellSouth was not easy. It is a great company filled with great people and I am proud to have been a part of its early years, but the prospects of being a part of the Olympic Games was too enticing to ignore. I decided to retire from the corporation and spend the final years of my career in the most exciting, exasperating, pressure-packed way possible.

To that end, I dutifully tape-recorded my activities while I was there. Each morning as I made my way to work (usually 5:00-5:30 AM) I would drive with one hand on the steering wheel and the other on the tape recorder. At the end of the day (usually 7:30-8:00 PM) I would do the same on the way home. I had assumed that the narratives might be of some interest to my four grandsons someday.

Once the Centennial Games were history, I filed away my notes and waited for someone to write a book on what happened in Atlanta—both the good and the bad. No one did. A chance conversation with my colleague and fellow columnist, Bill Shipp, led me to Mercer Press—and to you.

What you are about to read is my perspective, gleaned from those tapes and from the materials that I saved while there. This book is not a day-by-day account of what went on at the Atlanta Committee. There was not enough time to do that. It is my view, my opinions, and my reaction to how people and events impacted me.

You will also find a number of heroes on these pages. First and foremost is Billy Payne. I have been blessed to have known him and to have worked with him. I will try to explain him later in this book but suffice it to say, he is one of the most decent men I have ever known. Bob Holder, the man who convinced me to make the move from corporate America to the world of the Olympic Games, stayed close by. Whenever the pressure got too great or the task looked too futile, I could always count on him to get things back in perspective. He is a wise man.

I also count my colleagues at the senior management level as heroes. They were in an environment where they were constantly second-guessed and criticized, but they stayed the course and produced fine Games. I also have great admiration for all the people who comprised the ACOG family during the three and a half years I was privileged to be a part of them. Most of all, I salute the 50,000 volunteers who gave their time willingly and under some extreme conditions. They were living proof that "Southern Hospitality" is alive and well.

I do a lot of speaking around the country and one of the most frequent questions I get is, "Would you do it all over again?" The truth is, I don't know. My time at ACOG was filled with soaring highs and crushing lows. I made some great friends and have some wonderful memories, but I also have some regrets. There are things I wish I had done better. I may have made the same mistakes at BellSouth, but they were exacerbated in the intense public glare of the Olympics. I regret also that Atlanta didn't do better. The city couldn't live up to its hype and showed it to the whole world.

Your own opinions reflect what you saw and felt during those magical seventeen days that Atlanta hosted the world in 1996. What you haven't seen is how we did it—until now. I hope you enjoy this peek behind the curtain.

# 1

## THE BLAST HEARD AROUND THE WORLD

*"Explosion in Centennial Park:
At Least Two Dead"
Atlanta Journal Constitution, 7/28/96*

*The single most traumatic day of my 30 years in the business.*
—Diary Entry, July 27, 1996

It was the call that I had hoped would never come. At 1:40 AM on the morning of July 27, the midway point of the 1996 Centennial Olympic Games in Atlanta, I was wakened at home from a brief sleep by Richard Stogner, the duty officer in the Olympic Games Command Center. Stogner, a former City of Atlanta financial official, had joined the Atlanta Committee for the Olympic Games a year or so earlier to help guide us through the financial minefields of privately funding this $1.7 billion enterprise. He was one of several senior managers who rotated responsibility as duty officer in the high-tech Center, which monitored everything from the weather to traffic jams to ticket scalping.

"Dick, there has been an explosion in Centennial Park. There have been several deaths and we don't know how many injuries," he said calmly. Dumbfounded, all I could think to say in response was, "I'll be right there."

Today, as I reflect on that moment, I realize I had spent thirty-five years preparing for what would be the largest crisis of my career and the most intense twenty-four hours of my life. Everything I had learned and had practiced as a public relations professional would be put to the test by the Olympic Park bombing. The fact that I was one of the first to hear from Stogner was a testament to where the external environment stood in importance among the management of the Centennial Olympic Games. That I would sit at the table with a select group of senior managers and law enforcement officials and help plan our next moves was no accident. I had earned that right over the years with my insistence that external counsel is paramount in all decisions facing an organization. I like to think I was there also because there was confidence in my abilities on the part of all the parties around the table based on my track record of handling complex crises over my career.

Then there was my prickly personality that would have demanded a seat among the decision-makers, even had I not been invited. It would not have been the first time I forced my way into a meeting to insist on representation of external issues on pending decisions.

Getting to the table is one thing, but making a difference is something else. That was the challenge in the early morning hours of July 27.

In planning for the Olympics, we had tried to anticipate most of the issues that could likely occur during the Games, and my department had developed contingency plans to deal with them: hot weather, traffic gridlock, protests, logistics, unhappy customers, defecting athletes, the rumor de jour, and, of course, security.

Ironically, in pre-Game briefings with federal law enforcement officials, we had been assured that the Centennial Games should not be a target for international terrorism. Our government had gotten word to all nations, including the several with whom we have no diplomatic relations, to keep an eye on their extremist groups. If they didn't and someone tried to use our Games as the PLO had done in the Munich Olympics of 1972, the United States, as one FBI agent so eloquently put it, "will hurt you." While I had a good idea what that meant, I felt it wise to not ask.

Nor was there much concern for the militia types that are prevalent in the Southeast and Southwest. The feeling among the law enforcement agencies was that the United States athletes would do well in the Games (they did) and this would result in a lot of flag-waving and "USA! USA!" chants which would bring much pleasure to xenophobic militia groups. We were told by federal officials that if militia organizations tried to disrupt the Games, not only would they have the government after them, they would risk the wrath of other militia groups as well. Somehow, I felt that these people would rather have the Feds on their tail than fellow militia members.

However, in a comment that was to prove prescient, law enforcement officials said that no amount of security could prevent a random act of terrorism. Someone with a personal grudge, someone wanting to make a statement on a world stage, some deranged soul could simply place a bomb somewhere, walk away and wreak havoc. That was exactly what happened in Centennial Olympic Park that Saturday morning.

Throughout the Games and for the years preceding them, security was uppermost in our minds. Other than the financial pressures of raising money to host the Games, no issue consumed us more than security.

In early 1993, the Atlanta Committee had hired Bill Rathburn, chief of police in Dallas, Texas, to head security planning. As assistant chief of police in Los Angeles in 1984, Rathburn had been responsible for that city's Olympic security operations and had consulted with the government of South Korea on their security plans before the 1988 Games in Seoul, and with Spanish authorities in Barcelona before the 1992 Olympics. He was without question the most knowledgeable expert in the world on Olympic security.

Almost from the day he arrived in Atlanta, Rathburn had been concerned about security for the Games. Unlike Los Angeles, where the local police had provided the law enforcement support for the Games while still maintaining basic police services for the city, Atlanta did not have enough law enforcement officers to provide even a minimum level of support. The City of Atlanta police force was understaffed, underpaid and, to Rathburn's dismay, morale was rock bottom among the rank-and-file officers. During the Games, their performance was to be as poor as we had suspected it might be. But, no matter how good or bad the Atlanta police department, there simply were not enough bodies to do the job.

A much better law enforcement agency was the Georgia State Patrol but again, there were too few of them. Only 800 troopers were available to patrol the entire state of Georgia, let alone support the Atlanta Games. We would ask the state to supplement the GSP with a hodgepodge of personnel ranging from wildlife rangers to correction officers.

To cover the shortfall in people, our security plans called for a large contingent of military personnel and volunteers to do the basic non-law enforcement duties and thus free up peace officers to patrol the streets of Atlanta, the number two city for violent crime in the country in the mid-90's. We were asking the military to perform functions such as radio operations, manning magnetometers—the security devices that are used at all airport locations and would be used at our competition facilities—handbag searches, checking motor vehicles for bombs or suspicious packages, patrolling the perimeters of our facilities, and traffic control.

We were warned by friends in Congress and the Department of Defense not to place military personnel in inappropriate situations. Our chief critic, John McCain, the Republican senator from Arizona, had accused us of planning to use soldiers to wash the athletes's clothes, as well as cook and clean for them, none of which was true but which served to make security planning a high profile event among the national media that McCain so assiduously courted. (Ironically, when the blast did occur, most of the publicity-seekers like Senator McCain disappeared, not to be heard from again on the subject, leaving the Olympic Committee and the law enforcement agencies to sort through the rubble.)

I arrived at the parking entrance to Inforum, the headquarters of the Atlanta Olympic committee just as Billy Payne, ACOG's CEO, drove up. This turned out to be a fortunate turn of events because there was pandemonium around our building and across the street at Centennial Olympic Park. Grim-faced soldiers who approved access to our garage were not quite sure what to do. Reporters and photographers whose press center was also located in Inforum were shouting at anybody and at everybody. Police had emptied the building in search of additional bombs and the press could not get to their equipment and could get no answer as to when they would be allowed back in the building, while trying to cover a story of worldwide interest.

Payne's body guard/driver was Sgt. Bill Holton, on loan from the Georgia State Patrol. Holton, a soft-spoken gracious sort who could harden quickly, was busy getting Payne and me into the building and up to our offices on the sixth floor which overlooked the park. In spite of the chaos around us, nobody questioned Bill Holton who whispered a few words to the soldiers and to the police and then quietly waved us past the guards. I'm not sure that without Sgt. Holton's presence I could have gotten in the building that quickly.

We rode up the elevators together in complete silence. I was struck by Payne's demeanor. Normally high strung and excitable, he was noticeably quiet and had a trace of a smile on his face that I found odd. Today, I can only suppose what was going through his mind as we headed upstairs: nine years of labor, most of it in the face of criticism and doubt, fighting enemies real and imagined, bringing a miracle to his hometown, finally seeing his dream come to fruition, and then having this incomprehensible event occur in the park he had conceived. He, like the rest of us, was in a state of shock.

Centennial Olympic Park had been Billy Payne's proudest achievement surpassing, I believe, his having won the Games in the first place. Our offices were only a few feet from each other and had overlooked one of the seediest parts of the inner city: abandoned houses, overgrown vacant lots, empty businesses, half-occupied tenements, all within the shadow of the Coca-Cola Company's world headquarters. Every day, both Payne and I looked out our windows at the same scene and, yet, while the view never changed for me, the more he looked, the more a park emerged from his fertile imagination.

While the Park fell short of the size Payne had hoped, it was exactly what he had envisioned as a gathering place during the Games. Located on twenty-one acres and bounded by Coca-Cola Park, the Inforum building, the World Congress Center and Georgia Tech, it was a huge hit from the day it opened. Sponsors including AT&T, General Motors, Swatch, Anheuser Busch, and the State of Georgia located facilities in the park and large fountains provided a place for enthusiastic revelers to dance and soak themselves at the same time. During the Games, it is estimated that over 5.5 million people visited the park.

When Payne announced plans for the park in November 1993, it was a hit with the local newspaper, too. Much of their enthusiasm could be traced to the fact that its location was less than a mile from the paper's offices.

The Federal Reserve Bank and CNN were about the last business left in the Five Points area, which was once the center of Atlanta

5

commerce. Anything that improved the neighborhood would benefit them, as well.

But the Park was a logistical headache for ACOG's chief operating officer, A. D. Frazier. It disrupted the traffic flow and pick-up points for such key constituencies as the press. We were required to fence in the park to prevent spectators from piling into the streets where buses were running at the rate of one-per-minute. This brought howls from the local media as well as politicians after Rathburn opined that the fence would keep "undesirables" out. (Rathburn claimed a reporter had tricked him on a follow up call after an interview. The reporter claimed otherwise. It was one of the last times that anyone got interviewed by the media without someone from my staff present, much to the media's consternation.)

At Payne's insistence, the park was open until 2:00 AM each day. Those of us in a position to advise him warned him that this invited trouble. Closing at midnight would be the prudent thing to do, we said. As usual, he was right and we were wrong. The crowds were huge—averaging more that 300,000 people per day—but fun loving. They gathered to trade pins, romp in the fountains, enjoy the entertainment, or just enjoy each other. Unlike downtown Atlanta in pre-Olympic days, there were no instances of public drunkenness, pickpockets, fights, or unruly behavior of any kind in spite of the number of people who gathered daily. Everyone seemed intent on just having a good time.

The focal point of the park was AT&T's pavilion that featured live shows each evening as well as visits by Olympians. (One part of the pavilion had been reserved for Olympic athletes and their families to call home courtesy of the phone giant.) And it was on a spot nearby that someone placed the bomb heard round the world.

We gathered in A. D. Frazier's office at the other end of the building from Payne's. Frazier, the portly, acerbic, chain-smoking chief operating officer of ACOG was spending every night in his office, grabbing a few hours sleep on a sofa bed. Generally, he had a hard time sleeping because of the revelry in Centennial Park just below him. This morning, however, there was eerie silence, broken only by the squawk of emergency radios.

Payne, Frazier, and I walked out onto Frazier's balcony and surveyed the scene below us. Where only hours earlier, the park had been the site of constant festivity, now it was empty but for the police and emergency crews tending to the injured. The blue and lavender neon lights on the AT&T pavilion continued to sweep across the dark sky, giving the setting a strange, surreal quality. I looked down on a woman who was lying motionless on the ground with a blood-spattered blouse. Police shined a flashlight on her face before moving on. "She's dead," I told Payne. He nodded. Imagine my shock a few days later to see her picture in one of the national newspapers and to learn she wasn't even seriously injured!

Nobody said anything profound as we viewed the scene below us but inside we were all saying the same thing: Why? Why us?

By now it was 2:30 AM. Payne had called International Olympic Committee President Juan Antonio Samaranch to tell him what had happened and both agreed not to cancel nor delay the Games. It was obviously the correct decision but I felt it had been arrived at without much consideration of the unknowns. Was this the only bomb? Did we know who had planted it, and why? Was there a conspiracy involving the bombing of the US military barracks in Saudi Arabia a month earlier and the mysterious crash of the TWA jumbo jet over the waters of New York ten days ago? We didn't know. We could only deal with what we did know—the Centennial Games. Everything else we would leave to the law enforcement experts.

Payne returned to Frazier's office to find his chief operating officer talking simultaneously on the telephone and walkie-talkie, frantically trying to find someone who could let the press back into the building before there was a riot. My press relations representative, Bill Marks, had also been sleeping in his office each night and had gone downstairs immediately to try and get a handle on the situation. What he found was a media mob so angry that Marks thought for a moment they might take him hostage. He called Frazier appealing for help. The target of their wrath? A lone Atlanta policeman, a sergeant as I recall, standing guard at the entrance to the Main Press Center had said no one was coming back in and we were having a hard time finding anyone to countermand him. Finally, after a number of calls, Frazier finally found someone in authority that agreed to let the press back in the building. And just in the nick of time!

In the meantime, the Executive Management Team, made up of the most senior ACOG staff met in our sixth floor conference room with the

Mayor of Atlanta, Bill Campbell, members of the FBI, the Georgia Bureau of Investigation, and Francois Carrard, the director-general of the IOC and Samaranch's surrogate in the negotiations, to map out a strategy. Mack McLarty, President Clinton's longtime friend and our liaison with the White House, was in Atlanta and was keeping the president up-to-date on the situation. As soon as our meeting was over, McLarty, Payne, Frazier, Georgia Governor Zell Miller, and the Mayor briefed the president, who agreed with our decision to continue the Games.

Despite all that had happened just a few hours earlier, the group was strangely subdued. On a good day, ACOG was a frantic place in which to work. We were a group of Type-A workaholics faced with impossible deadlines, running, yelling, cursing ourselves, and screaming at each other. Time was always our enemy. There was never enough of it. Now facing the biggest crisis of the Games, everyone seemed almost serene. I would credit the difference to shock and fatigue except that good, practical decisions were being made quickly and decisively.

We all agreed that we must hold a press briefing as soon as possible and that 6:00 AM would be the best time for meeting the media. Payne asked me to draw up a plan on how to announce publicly that the Games would continue. Because the press had been so preoccupied with gaining entry back into the main press center, we had bought an hour or so to plan our next steps, but we were living on borrowed time. We had to tell them something quickly and show them, we hoped, that we were going to be as forthright as possible. Any delay because we couldn't get our act together would serve only to increase the media's frenzy and to make our collective jobs even more difficult. To everyone's credit, there was no one—Olympic official or law enforcement agency—advocating any delay.

The strategy was simple. Payne, one of the few people I met in the Olympic movement who believed in its innate goodness, would go on all the major networks, starting with our rights holder, NBC, and announce our decision to continue the Games. He would convey three messages: First, sympathy for the victims of the bombing. By now we had fairly conclusive information that one person had been killed in the bombing and one person, a Turkish cameraman, had died of a heart attack as he hurried to film the action. We were not quite sure how many were injured but we knew it was in the neighborhood of 100 or so. (A later report put the injured at 110.) Second, the Games were not going to be held hostage to terrorism of any form; third, the incident demonstrated vividly the unending need for the power of the Olympic movement. Payne was faithful to the message strategy and magnificent in the delivery. It was one of his finest moments. I could only imagine what he was feeling inside.

At the same time, Frazier would conduct morning and afternoon media briefings and use these sessions to assure the public that the Games would stay on schedule. He would do this by presenting the day's logistics: number of bus routes planned that day, number of riders, number of volunteers, number of competitions scheduled, attendance at the various competitions, tickets projected to be sold that day for future events, etc. He would return in the evening and compare what had been forecast with what had actually happened.

We often kidded Frazier, a former banker, that he never met a factoid he did not fall in love with, but this was one time when a calm recitation of numbers would give a sense of "business as usual" just when we needed it most.

As I was in awe of Billy Payne's enormous creative talents, I was just as amazed by A. D. Frazier's ability to keep up with the extraordinary details that went into operating the largest Olympic Games in history. Looking back on those days, I am convinced that not one of the many experts who reported to him knew more about their particular area than Frazier knew about it. He was like a sponge.

In his own way, Frazier was just as impressive and just as believable as Payne. The first briefing began around 6:00 AM to a standing room only audience. Frazier bravely predicted what would happen that day logistically. At around 4:00 PM, we held the second briefing and tallied the results. By the morning of the fourth day, there were so few media present that we decided to cancel the remaining briefings. Clearly, we had made our point that the Games were operating normally. What I wrote out that morning for Payne, Frazier, and the others was about a page and a half. If need be, we could change the plan with changing conditions. That never became necessary. We had scored a bulls-eye. I believe strongly in simple, concise messages, no matter how critical the situation. At a time of crisis, you want to speak within carefully-defined legal parameters, but that doesn't mean subjecting the public to "legal-speak." In a crisis like the bombing, you must communicate to your audiences with a few easily understood messages. It worked superbly as we sought to assure the world that the Games would go on.

Our plans also included separating the bombing issue from the Games. We would not talk about the investigation and leave that to the law enforcement authorities, with the FBI as the lead agency. This decision caused a major screw-up for which I hold myself responsible.

Unlike the press, broadcasters buy the rights to the Games and get credentials allowing them more access than their non-rights holder colleagues receive, a privilege they guard jealously. Credentials admit the holder into press briefings, interview rooms, media lounges, etc. Because of the obvious interest in the subject, I had requested that the FBI hold their briefings "off premise" to allow media coverage without worrying about what individual was credentialed to attend the event. Because we could not find a suitable location nearby, we had no choice but to hold the security briefings in our Main Press Center. When CNN, ABC, CBS, and other broadcasters sent news reporters to Inforum, they were turned away because they were not credentialed. Only their sports personnel were and these people were not seen by the networks as qualified to cover something as major as the park bombing.

We took a lot of justifiable criticism for our inability to move quickly enough to grant these additional credentials. We later got the kinks smoothed out but the media were not in a forgiving mood and cited this as another example of Southern inefficiency.

By 9:00 AM, everything was in place. The first briefings had taken place and the world knew the Centennial Olympic Games would continue. There was one overarching concern: Would anyone actually show up for the Games that day? What about the athletes? Spectators? Volunteers? We could only wait until the morning competitions began to see if the bombing had permanently chilled the enthusiasm that had been built up over the past seven days. This was a stark reminder that no matter how much experience one has in the external environment and no matter how solid the crisis plan, no one can predict public reaction.

Scott Anderson, who as Games Services managing director was in charge of ticket sales, hotel reservations, food service, along with a myriad of other duties, was out in the city awaiting the results of our collective efforts. About 11:00 AM, he called half laughing, half crying.

"Dick, it is unbelievable!" he said, "Crowds are streaming into the stadium and we've got a full volunteer contingent."

That was only the beginning of the good news. By the end of the day, we had held twenty-one competitions. Our stadiums operated at 95% capacity and over 85% of our volunteers showed up for duty. The most telling statistic, however, was in the sale of future day tickets. We had devised a plan where at any venue, spectators could buy available tickets to any future competitions at any other venue. This had proven an extremely popular and profitable process. On the previous days, we had sold some 35,000 tickets to future events. Less than twenty-four hours after the bombing, we sold 27,000 additional tickets.

The fans had answered the anonymous bomber in the best way they knew how: Let the Games go on.

The days to follow would find Richard Jewell accused of the bombing (and later exonerated), the media engaged in a shameful display of one-upsmanship that cost several news organizations big dollars by their zeal to "beat the competition" and with others yet to face the piper, the FBI going from hero to goat, and the initial reluctance of security officials to okay reopening the park. Yet, by Tuesday all signals were "go." How to open the park with sensitivity after what had occurred just a few days earlier and then how get us back to the excitement and friendship that had been so evident before the explosion was a long and sometimes heated debate. But, we did it. Along with the lighting of the Olympic flame in the temple in Olympia, Greece, it was the most emotional moment I had experienced in my career. Andrew Young, Atlanta's former mayor and co-chairman of our board, delivered perhaps his greatest sermon ever, which, if you have ever had the privilege of hearing him speak, is saying a lot. On the day the park reopened, more than 40,000 people gathered to sing and pray and cry and hug. Before the day was over, some 250,000 visited the park. We were truly back in business.

As you read this, the bomber, now assumed to be Eric Rudolph, still has not been brought to justice and may not even be alive. Why our government with all the resources at its disposal, has been unable to find him is baffling to me. Before the Games, I was absolutely convinced that no one could do what was done in Centennial Park and get away with it. Sadly, that appears to have happened.

As I look back with the perspective of several years behind me, a number of things stick out in my mind. First, no one asked to see my plan for conveying to the public that the Games would continue. No lawyers nor law enforcement agencies, nobody at the White House, or the State Capitol, or City Hall, or within ACOG questioned me about what I was going to do or what I proposed to say. I cannot really explain that phenomenon except that most of the people in the room knew me, respected me, trusted me, and had too many other pressing issues to deal with. I had spent thirty-five years of "on-the-job"'training for that moment and I believe everyone assumed that based on my track record, I would do the right thing. That was a leap of faith that few public relations people have ever experienced, although I was too busy at the time to focus on it.

Second, no one knew what the public's reaction to our decision to continue the Games would be. The fact that we received such a positive response was a testimony as much to people's revulsion at such a cowardly act as to anything the Committee did. I think we just gave them a good reason to express their defiance. A makeshift sign in the park perhaps said it best: "The World's Heart Cried for a Nite, but You Didn't Break It." The Centennial Olympic Games would continue without missing a beat.

If the bomber had intended otherwise, he had failed.

# 2

## Boiling Over:
## Life in the Pressure Cooker

There is an old saying that two things you never want to see being made are law and sausage. To that I would add a third: Olympic planning. It's not very pretty.

Strangely, there seems to be little that can be learned from previous Olympic Games. Each host city is different. Moscow, Los Angeles, Seoul, and Barcelona have little in common with Atlanta, Georgia. The governments are different, the terms and conditions by which the Games were secured are different, and the people running them are different. In fact, about the only thing consistent is that every host city vows not to make the same mistakes their predecessors made, promptly proceeds to do so, and adds a few new ones for good measure.

Only on the field of play is there uniformity. One hundred meters is one hundred meters, no matter where the Olympic Games are held. When an athlete steps onto a field of play, there can be no variation in the conditions under which he or she competes. But getting there requires a lot of "make it up as you go along."

One of the rationales I used in deciding to retire early from what was arguably the best public relations job in America and join the Atlanta Committee for the Olympic Games—besides being a native Atlantan and wanting to give something back to my hometown—was that I had been deeply involved in the divestiture of the Bell System some ten years earlier. I had been fortunate to play a role in the formation of one of the "Baby Bells" spawned from the breakup, BellSouth Corporation. I was familiar with and comfortable in an environment of complexity and uncertainty. There was no question that there would be large amounts of both at ACOG.

As I would learn, however, the difference in dismantling the largest corporation in the world and creating the largest peacetime event in history, as it was often described by Billy Payne, was the difference in butter and butterfly. What I had failed to take into account was that the divestiture of the Bell System and the creation of the Baby Bells were managed by a group of people who had worked together for years, even decades. We used the same technology, the same systems, the same terminology, and whether in Minnesota or South Carolina, we were of a singular corporate culture nurtured for more than a century by Ma Bell. As traumatic as divestiture was for all of us who had grown up in the Bell System, the planning was thoughtful, thorough, and dignified. I can't recall a single instance of anyone's losing his or her temper at a fellow team member during the two years of divestiture planning.

The Atlanta Committee for the Olympic Games could not have been more different. There is no preexisting culture in an Olympic Games planning committee. In Atlanta, everyone on the senior management team was from somewhere else and had brought his or her own management style, experiences, culture, personal quirks, biases, and egos with them. Shyness and a lack of strong opinions were in short supply. Everybody was used to being *the* leader. If you weren't supremely self-confident, you wouldn't last long at ACOG.

Our impossible deadlines made niceties an unaffordable luxury. There was simply too much to do and much too little time in which to get it done. You said what was on your mind and had to expect responses that would be just as direct in return. To an outsider, it had to be a frightening experience to sit in on a senior management meeting and wonder if someone was going to kill a colleague halfway through the agenda.

The quality of people who answer the siren call of the Olympics is amazing and Atlanta was no exception. I'm not sure why the allure. In my case, I thought I was doing something for Atlanta. I can only assume for the others that it was the opportunity to be a part of history, to be able to say, "I was there." Give this to the Olympic movement: it is the grandest show on earth in terms of raw emotion, human triumph, and celebration. What it takes to get to that point, however, is not very inspiring. The years before the Games begin are filled with money concerns, petty politics, media sniping, and special interests pressures. It takes an exceptional management to survive and the Atlanta Committee for the Olympic Games had it.

Almost without exception, people considered at the top of their field headed every discipline at the committee. For example, heading security planning was Bill Rathburn, former chief of police in Dallas, Texas, and in charge of the Los Angeles police contingent at the Los Angeles Games in 1984. It was Rathburn's job to coordinate the efforts among many law enforcement support from the cities and counties hosting various Olympic events as well as state and federal personnel. Unlike the rest of the world, we don't have a national police force. Our Constitution won't allow it. Our system of government puts law enforcement at the local level. Good idea for democracy but a major headache when putting on an event the size of the Olympics. The result is a jumble of agencies, some with overlapping authority, some more proficient than others, but all managing one of the most critical functions of any Olympic Games — security. It was a frustrating job even before the park bombing.

The managing director of sports was Dave Maggard, former athletic director at the University of Miami, Florida, and a former Olympian himself. Ultimately, the success of the 1996 Centennial Olympic Games would depend in large part on his organization because after all the controversies, monies, egos, politics, and posturing had been dealt with, the world's attention would turn to sports. Maggard had to get 10,000 athletes from 197 countries — 80% of whom would be eliminated in the first round — to their field of play on time, give them ideal conditions in which to compete and ensure that everything ran smoothly for the sixteen days of competition. There is no question that the best-managed Olympic organization in the world will be remembered as the worst if the athletic competition is flawed. With perhaps the smallest ego of the senior management, Maggard was ideal to deal with the international sporting federations — from archery to yachting — who felt their sport was the most important in the Games, and the facilities in which they were to compete were the least adequate.

Dealing with the whining and complaining from the federations as well as the national Olympic committees and the IOC, I am convinced, would have caused Job to throw up his hands and quit, but Maggard exhibited enormous patience with these prima donnas and was successful in his mission. Before the athletes were through in Atlanta, they had set 662 records, including thirty-two world records and 111 Olympic records. It didn't hurt that many of those records came at the hands of the U.S. Olympians.

Scott Anderson was in charge of Games Services, which included ticket sales, concession sales, and accommodations. Anderson had been president of Callaway Gardens, a popular resort near Columbus, Georgia, and before that an hotelier for a number of years. His responsibilities were daunting, to say the least. The Atlanta Committee put on sale 11 million tickets—more than Los Angeles and Barcelona combined—and needed to sell at least 60% of them to generate the $261 million we had forecasted toward the $1.7 billion budget. Of course, selling tickets to opening and closing ceremonies would be a snap, but we also had to sell tickets to modern pentathlon, fencing, and field hockey. We also had preliminary soccer matches scheduled for Washington, DC, Orlando, and Miami, Florida, and Birmingham, Alabama, in football stadiums that would seat from 60,000 to 80,000 people. There were plenty of tickets available and they would be conveniently priced but making the budget was the issue.

After the tickets were sold, our visitors needed a place to stay, as did the 15,000 media, our sponsors and their guests. The International Olympic poobahs had already taken care of their own creature comforts and had selected the posh Marriott Marquis as their home away from home. Sorting out who stayed where also fell in Anderson's bailiwick. He had some 1,300 hotels with over 100,000 rooms in his inventory. His job wasn't made easier by the fact that many of the accommodations being offered were in an 18-county area and some as much as 35-40 miles out of town. (It is interesting to note how Atlanta defines itself. It can be as small as the city limits, which encompasses about 400,000 people or as large as twenty counties and three million people, depending on what kind of point we are trying to make.) Located on the eastern seaboard, Atlanta is within two hours flying time of half the population of the United States. We had priced the tickets affordably. We were expecting a crowd, and we got one.

Payne had pledged that no government funds would be used in putting on the Games (or, "inside the fence" as we referred to it) and our agreement with the City of Atlanta indemnified it from any tax liabilities. There was no guaranteed government safety net under us: a fact that the International Olympic Committee vowed would never be allowed to happen again in the awarding of the Games. The IOC was rightfully concerned that if we didn't raise all the money necessary, we would have to reduce the scope of the Games and cut corners on some of the creature comforts—arm rests in the stadium seats, bare concrete where there should be carpeting, bare walls where there should be paint. Cut-rate Games were not what they were looking for when they awarded Atlanta the centennial celebration of the modern Olympics.

That meant an aggressive effort to raise the necessary $1.7 billion from private sources. Of that amount, one third of the proposed revenues was budgeted to come from sponsorships. The other two-thirds were to come equally from television rights sales and the ticket sales with some "all other" thrown in. Sponsors were being asked to pay $40 million, more than ten times what the Los Angeles Olympic Games sponsorships had cost. Of course, the Atlanta Games were roughly twice as large as LA's had been. In addition, there were licensees for everything from Olympic pins to clothing to game shows. (*Jeopardy* was the official game show sponsor.)

Marketing the Atlanta Games was accomplished through a joint venture between the Atlanta Committee and the United States Olympic Committee, called the Atlanta Centennial Olympic Properties or ACOP. This was something new. The rationale for the joint venture was that instead of competing for dollars, the U.S. Committee and the Atlanta Committee would sign one sponsor who would have ties to both organizations. These corporations would not only be an Atlanta Games sponsor, but also would be associated with the U.S. teams as well.

Managing this complicated process was Bill McCahan, a retired IBM marketing executive. While we could all lay claim to the hardest job in the organization, an objective third-party might have awarded that title to McCahan hands down. Not only was he dealing with a hand-wringing management anxious for some cash, he was dealing with sponsors who wanted to be assured they would be getting the maximum bang for the buck they were putting in the enterprise. Sometimes it was hard to recognize our friends from our foes. While the USOC was our partner, they had a long-term view of the Olympic Games since they had been around for a lot of them and planned to be around for a lot more. We burst on the scene in time to put on the 1996 Games and were trying to get through the closing ceremonies with all our bills paid. To say we had a short-term view was an understatement. As with Rod Tidwell, Cuba Gooding's character in the hit movie, *Jerry Maguire*, our philosophy was, "Show me the money."

A third party in the marketing equation was, of course, the International Olympic Committee, who sold sponsorships to corporations wanting worldwide exposure, which included the Coca-Cola Company and UPS, both Atlanta firms, as well as IBM, Kodak, Xerox, Visa, Panasonic, Bausch & Lomb, and John Hancock. One of the myths of the Atlanta Olympic Games was that Coca-Cola somehow had "bought" the Centennial Games for Atlanta. Look at Coke's marketplace. It is much larger than Atlanta and there was no way they were going to offend their markets around the world by playing favorites. In addition, the fact that the company made a deal with the IOC meant that the sponsorship was shared with a number of national Olympic committees around the world. Our take was only 36% of the total.

One of McCahan's' perennial headaches was ambush marketing, a super-sophisticated process where companies competitive with Olympic sponsors create advertising that makes them look like they are a part of the Olympic Games when in fact they are not. We were prepared for the American Expresses of the world, but we had not counted on one of our biggest potential ambushers — the City of Atlanta.

Constructing the facilities was the most high profile and critical of all the jobs, prior to the Games. It was where the bulk of the money went and where the greatest likelihood of cost overruns would occur. Billy Payne, ACOG's founder and CEO, had decreed that, where possible, the facilities in Atlanta would be built for life after the Games and then retrofitted for use during the Olympics. This was exactly the opposite of the way past Olympic committees had operated and would ensure that Atlanta did not end up with a number of white elephant structures that would be of little practical use after the Games. After the Atlanta Olympics, the facilities would be given to the various cities, universities, and sporting authorities free of charge. This included the baseball stadium for the Atlanta Braves, who were threatening to leave downtown Atlanta without someone—they didn't care who—building them a new one.

This was one of Payne's best ideas and one that will long outlive the traumas of putting on the Olympics in Atlanta. But it meant building a 45,000-seat baseball stadium, for example, and then retrofitting it to be an 85,000-seat stadium for track and field and the opening and closing ceremonies; or constructing a 3,000-seat aquatic center at Georgia Tech, recognizing that college swimming is a minor sport and converting it temporarily into a 16,000-seat stadium for the Olympic Games, where swimming is one of the marquee events.

This task fell to Bill Moss, a quiet, no-nonsense type who had been involved in the construction of Disney's Epcot Center in Orlando and the Universal Studios there. Of all the hires at ACOG, Moss was probably the most valuable. I am convinced that no one else could have handled his job. Moss had to build the facilities while contending with funding problems, union issues, special interest groups, media scrutiny, and a City of Atlanta that was less than cooperative. To me it is amazing that his organization was never charged with favoritism, accused of unfair practices by minority firms anxious to get in on this one-time largesse, or found to be cutting corners in a tough financial environment. He did his job on time and on budget. To my way of thinking, Bill Moss never got the credit he deserved for his contributions to the 1996 Games. They were significant.

Relationships with the City of Atlanta fell to Shirley Franklin, former chief of staff to Mayor Andrew Young and predicted to be the next mayor of Atlanta. She was the point person with the politically divisive, racially charged leaders at City Hall. One of our biggest challenges was our city services contract. As with the other governmental agencies where we were holding competitions, we had to negotiate on what services they would provide and what we would pay for. The largest contract, of course, was with the City of Atlanta. Because of the huge financial benefit the Games would bring to Atlanta, Dick Pound, chair of the coordination commission set up by the IOC to oversee our progress, expressed some hope that the city might want to donate their services to ACOG. Fat chance. Even though estimates put that financial benefit at some $200 million, if anyone thought the city was going to be our partner in putting on the Games, they were in for a shock. Atlanta city government viewed the Centennial Games as a chance to get rich. The city services contract was just one opportunity.

The job of running the massive host broadcasting operations that would provide the broadcast signal to some 3 billion people in over 214 countries and territories around the world was in the hands of Manolo Romero, a Spaniard who had done the Barcelona Games and numerous World Cup competitions and was considered the singular expert in his field. Unlike the rest of us, Romero knew exactly where his next job would be. He would be headed to the next World Cup.

The modern Olympics are television games. Much is still made by the IOC as to the importance of the press (and much is made by the press of the importance of the press). Don't believe it. One lesson I was to learn is that the press seem to talk to themselves a lot. But it is television that creates the lasting image of the Olympic Games.

At one point we were worried about the possibility of a hot, steamy Georgia summer while the athletes and spectators were in town. Atlanta temperatures can easily get to 100° at that time of the year and I knew that would give the national and international press another excuse to decry the selection of this deep South city to host the 1996 Games. I mentioned this to Dick Ebersol, president of NBC Sports, our television rights holder in the United States. "Do you remember watching the Lions and the Packers in the old days on television?" he asked. "Never missed it," I said. "Well," Ebersol said, "Did you care how cold it was in Green Bay, as you sat in your easy chair after a Thanksgiving meal? Did that affect your enjoyment of the game?" "Absolutely not," I replied.

He said, "The three billion people watching these Games around the world aren't going to care how hot it is in Atlanta, either. Just get the athletes to their competitions on time. That they will care about. Forget the rest of it." I did not have to test his theory, because thankfully we had excellent weather, but his point was an excellent one. I never cared what the weather was as I watched football on television and the world wasn't going to care about it as they tuned in to the Olympic Games.


Enforcing financial discipline in an organization like ACOG was like trying to herd cats through a keyhole. Patrick Glisson had been the City of Atlanta's chief financial officer and assumed that same role at ACOG.

When you are trying to welcome the world and put on the largest Olympic Games ever held and do it all in grand style, the last thing you want to be told is, "We can't afford it." But that was Pat's job and he was usually right. We couldn't afford it. Seeing Glisson come into your office was akin to a drop-in visit from the Internal Revenue Service. It probably wasn't going to be good news. Needless to say, you couldn't have given me his job but he handled a tough and controversial assignment professionally and with good humor and got us out of there with no red ink.

Dr. Sherman Day, a respected educator, supervised the construction and development of Centennial Olympic Park. He is a kind and gentle man and was a favorite of Georgia Governor Zell Miller and his staff. Dr. Day was usually able to test the "temperature" of the governor and let us know if we were heading in or out of his doghouse. He was as easy going as Billy Payne was intense, yet both suffered heart problems while we were in the planning stages and both, thankfully, recovered to enjoy the fruits of their labors.

Doris Isaac-Stallworth, a former IBMer, had the unenviable job of trying to manage a human resources function in this mad house. Remember, the Atlanta Committee started with a handful of people in 1991 and grew to over 50,000 in just five years. Every department head, including me, needed everybody right now. Forget background checks, budgets, training, office space, and computers. Just get me the people. Hers was one of the most thankless job in the place, including Glisson's.

There were to be additional hires of equally talented people at the senior level as the planning process moved along, and I will refer to some of them elsewhere but this was the group that I joined in January of 1993. In retrospect, it was a helluva team.

As talented as this management team was, we were the "outsiders," — people who were not an integral part of the group that had secured the 1996 Centennial Olympic Games for Atlanta. That assemblage originally numbered ten people and four of them, Payne, Ginger Watkins, Linda Stephenson, and Charlie Battle, took full-time positions with the planning committee.

In doing so, they were immediate targets for the media, who questioned their ability to operate such a complicated organization with no previous management experience. I found that concern unfounded because while none of them had much corporate experience, they knew the Olympic movement inside out, and that certainly counted for something. But it never stopped the sniping from the media and some of the "outsiders."

Payne, of course, became chief executive officer and, to my knowledge, is the only bid committee chairman who ever functioned as CEO through the end of the Games.

Watkins, a community volunteer who had supervised the public relations function before I came on board, was in charge of the opening and closing ceremonies, the torch relay, the "look" of the Games, and was Payne's closest confidant. Her curt manner didn't make her popular with a lot of people within the committee but I found her very capable.

Stephenson, also a community volunteer, supervised the Cultural Olympiad—an event that even without the Olympic Games would have been a huge event on its own—and the all-important volunteer training. We were counting on some 50,000 volunteers to work in a variety of jobs ranging from squiring VIP's around town to sweeping out stables at the Equestrian Center.

Battle, bond attorney, was the liaison with the International Olympic Committee, the individual country Olympic organizations and the national governing bodies that supervise the individual sports that compete in the Games. He was without doubt, the best-liked person in the Olympic movement. In an imperialistic environment that fostered backbiting, cliques and cabals, I never met anyone in the Olympics who didn't like Charlie Battle. It was quite extraordinary.

These were the "insiders."

Before assuming what would be at Games time a mid-size Fortune 500 company in terms of assets, Payne had been a real estate attorney with no corporate management experience. Even the most senior and experienced officers I had known in my own corporate life would have had a hard time keeping up with the details of this enterprise. The organization would grow from ten people to 104,000—including volunteers—in less than six years. It would go from no assets to near $1.7 billion, would operate for three weeks, and then disappear.

More importantly, since Payne was so closely identified with the whole effort, the success or failure of the Games would be his. Because he was sensitive to the doubters who thought the job too big for him, he tended to get involved in every detail of every job. His creativity was something to marvel at and there wasn't much that couldn't be made better by his participation, but the operation was too complex for any one person—be it Peter Ueberroth or Billy Payne—to manage.

The first to recognize this was ACOG's co-chairman Bob Holder, chairman and CEO of a large and highly successful construction firm in Atlanta. Holder met Payne while chairman of the Atlanta Chamber of Commerce, heard of the plans to bid for the 1996 Olympic Games, and supported the effort financially and through his contacts in the business community. Because of the respect that his business colleagues hold for him, Bob Holder brought immediate respectability and dollars to Payne's efforts. He convinced Atlanta corporations to ante up $200,000 each to help fund the $7.5 million needed to conduct the bid campaign and became a good friend of IOC president Juan Antonio Samaranch. A quintessential Southern gentleman, Bob Holder could be tough when he had to. Not satisfied with ACOG's external image, he convinced me to retire from BellSouth and join the team.

Holder recognized in the earliest days of the organization the need for an experienced chief operating officer to run the day-to-day details and free Payne do what he did best: focus on the big picture, maintain the relationship with Samaranch and the other Olympic leaders, inspire and motivate the team (perhaps his most important responsibility), and stay out of the details of organizing the Games.

A. D. Frazier, executive vice president of First Chicago Bank, was selected to serve as the organization's chief operating officer. Frazier had strong ties to Atlanta. As a young banker, he had been involved in the gubernatorial campaign of Jimmy Carter. When Carter became president, Frazier was selected to handle all the inaugural festivities and then became number two in the Office of Management and Budget, working for chairman and Carter ally Bert Lance.

Lance lasted only a short while and left. A disillusioned Frazier wasn't far behind, ending up in Chicago. He jumped at the chance to return to Atlanta.

He was perfectly suited to convert Payne's dreams to bricks and mortars. While Billy had brought the vision, A. D.'s job was to make it happen.

Of the senior management, Watkins, McCahan, and I reported directly to Payne. The rest of the staff, including "insiders" Battle and Stephenson, reported to Frazier, although our responsibilities required that we all stay in close touch. A. D. held a staff meeting every Monday morning. Everybody around the table would update the group on their particular issues. It was always amazing to me that before the meeting was over, it had engendered a number of side meetings. Three people would gather in the corner and get closure to an issue. Two would leave to be replaced by another two who would address a totally different matter. On and on it would go. At the risk of exaggeration, you tried to go to the men's room during the staff meeting, not afterward. Otherwise, you would find yourself in a lengthy ad hoc meeting, which was not your original purpose for being there.

Payne and Frazier were truly the odd couple. Payne was big picture and a true visionary. Frazier had an enormous capacity for detail. Payne's focus was short and intense; Frazier's long and sometime laborious. His staff joked that "A. D." stood for "All Day" Frazier because of the length of his meetings. Actually, his name was Adolphus Drewry. Both were extremely complicated and except for sometimes overlapping job responsibilities, the two men were a perfect match and very loyal to each other. While both would deny it, each liked to dabble in the other's business. Payne had a habit of calling whomever he wanted for whatever he needed, no matter where in the business they happened to work and giving an order for something he wanted done. Many times, he forgot to tell Frazier, who would be infuriated by Payne's end run.

Frazier, on the other hand, enjoyed the external exposure that was primarily Payne's responsibility. Highly outspoken and, thus, highly quotable, he was a favorite of the media. He was also very credible with them because he knew the operations of this complex organization like the back of his hand. It placed me in a delicate position when Payne would pick up the paper and see Frazier quoted in a story on ACOG. There were times it was more appropriate for A. D. to be talking to the media than for Billy but it was a constant balancing act. The local paper became convinced that Billy was some kind of Elmer Gantry, mistaking his enthusiasm for hyperbole, and that the "truth" lay with A. D. For example, when Payne announced that dormitory construction was on schedule, Melissa Turner, a reporter at the *Atlanta Constitution*, demanded to talk to Frazier and find out "what the real truth was." The real truth was that the dormitory construction was on schedule as Payne had said. I suggested to Frazier that he call her off line and tell her that his job was to implement whatever the CEO told him to. To his credit, he did that.

It wasn't in my job description but when either got in the other's business I found myself relaying messages from one to the other to either notify them of the fact or to say, "Keep out." Payne and Frazier met several times a day to discuss a myriad of details but evidently "encroachment" was never on their agenda. I sometimes felt like Henry Kissinger running a diplomatic mission.

On one occasion, A. D. hit the ceiling when he found out that Dave Maggard, who reported to him, was meeting with Billy and former Atlanta Falcons football coach Leeman Bennett without Frazier's knowledge. He was understandably furious. At the same time that he was glowering over the latest violation in internal protocol, he himself had been invited to be a part of a CEO-to-CEO road show sponsored by IBM. It was too prestigious an opportunity to turn down but he wasn't the CEO, he was chief operating officer. So he asked me to brief Billy on his accepting the invitation. I can only surmise that my being in the middle would keep both of them from having a major confrontation over what the other one was doing.

Despite the strong and talented personalities that populated the Atlanta Committee, we were not as independent in our decision-making as we tried to tell ourselves we were. We received additional management oversight from ACOG's thirty-one member board of directors, composed of business leaders, neighborhood activists, labor, representatives of the IOC and the United States Olympic Committee, appointees from the State of Georgia and the City of Atlanta, plus the "insiders" Payne, Battle, Stephenson, Watkins, Horace Sibley, one of the original members of the bid committee and a partner in the King & Spalding law firm, who also served as our legal counsel, and Bobby Reardon, another of the original volunteers. Co-chaired by Bob Holder and former Atlanta mayor and civil rights hero Andrew Young, the board served as a good sounding board for management. The *Atlanta Journal-Constitution* never gave the board credit for the leadership it provided us but rather, deemed it a rubber-stamp for whatever Billy Payne wanted to do. At the same time, the same reporters were convinced that Billy really wasn't running the organization; it was A. D. Frazier.

However, it was the Metropolitan Atlanta Olympic Games Authority that wielded the most clout over our operation. The Georgia Legislature had formed MAOGA because the state constitution prohibited the city of Atlanta from entering into multi-year construction contracts. Thus, the authority was formed. Under an agreement between MAOGA, the city of Atlanta and the Atlanta Committee for the Olympic Games—called the Tri-Party Agreement—MAOGA would assume the obligations required by the IOC and then transfer those obligations to ACOG. In turn, the committee would indemnify the city and the state of any Games-related financial liabilities.

At its inception, it was composed of the mayor of Atlanta, the president of the Atlanta City Council, and three people appointed by the mayor. The agency was expanded to twelve people to include representation from the state and from Fulton County. For some months, it wasn't clear how the agency would function and it was slow in getting its act together. It did not help that the twelve-person Authority hired a former Newark, New Jersey city manager, Richard Monteilh (pronounced MON-tay), as executive director who proceeded to announce to the world that MAOGA was the official host under the IOC agreement. "We subcontracted with ACOG. If we lose confidence in ACOG's numbers, then we have the right to bring in another committee," Monteilh told the media. That was factually incorrect and politically naïve, as he was to learn in the firestorm that followed.

At this point George Berry, former commissioner of Atlanta's Aviation Department and later commissioner of the Georgia Department of Industry and Trade stepped in as chairman. Berry was all business and had little interest in the Games themselves as he told Payne and Frazier. With the backing and confidence of the governor and the mayor (a rather rare occurrence), Berry and MAOGA would closely monitor the Atlanta Committee's financial health. Raising money in the private sector and assuring there would be enough to construct necessary facilities was going to require close scrutiny. No one wanted a financial debacle as had occurred in Montreal twenty years earlier. There, taxpayers ended up with a debt of over one billion dollars. Berry was determined to see that private Games remained private and that if tax dollars were going to be impacted, there would be an organization to monitor why and how much. To that end, MAOGA retained an accounting firm to audit us and to ensure there indeed would be no financial liabilities.

The Authority's oversight was Payne's first hard lesson to learn. When he had won the Games for Atlanta, he had basically given up control of them. From now on, he could not do just what he wanted to do as he had done while directing the bid strategy. He now could do only what the various interest groups, including MAOGA, would permit him to do. He never quite came to terms with that harsh reality.

As tough-minded and as confident of our individual abilities as we all were, the pressures of an environment where everything is magnified beyond recognition, with deadlines piled on top of deadlines, where efforts to raise almost $2 billion must be timed with a construction program that won't allow any delays will finally break even the most resilient among us. I speak from experience. I resigned twice in frustration. A. D. Frazier resigned once, and two of the senior managers were ready to duke it out publicly.

It was the week before Christmas 1995. While everyone else seemed to be getting ready for Peace on Earth, we were being treated to the spectacle of a normally kind and gentle Dave Maggard losing his cool in a staff meeting and inviting Scott Anderson to meet him on the loading dock to settle their differences. The cause of the dispute? Anderson had insisted that Maggard write a letter to the international sporting federations demanding immediate payment if the federations wanted their accommodations guaranteed. By this time, finding enough rooms to meet the demand was becoming critical. If the federations didn't turn in their monies soon, Anderson was going to take their rooms and give them to someone else, like sponsors or the media. It turned out, however, that most of the federations had already paid and were furious with Maggard for suggesting they had not. This had caused Maggard terrible political problems with a very influential group within the Olympic movement. He came to the meeting embarrassed and angry with Anderson. Anderson didn't seem very contrite about the matter. Extremely strong words were exchanged between the two and Maggard issued his invitation. Obviously, Maggard was exhausted like the rest of us, for it was completely unlike him to do such a thing. He was one of the nicest people in the organization. It was also obvious that Anderson was also tired, otherwise no one in their right mind would have ever dreamed of meeting Maggard on a loading dock or anywhere else. Maggard, in his mid-50's, still looked fit enough to put anyone he chose on their butt, as he had done as a linebacker at Cal some years back. To make matters even more ludicrous, Anderson had a broken foot and was in an ankle cast. So, as Maggard stormed out of the room and headed for the loading dock some six floors below, Anderson came gimping out like Walter Brennan on the *Real McCoys*. Fortunately, everyone cooled off, fisticuffs were avoided, and, as was the nature of our organization, the episode was totally forgotten and it seems to never have affected the relationship between Maggard and Anderson. But that incident was indicative of the stress we were feeling as the Games approached.

I had fallen victim to the pressure a couple of times and had quit. The first time was in early February 1994, just before the Winter Olympics in Lillehammer, Norway. We had just finished a very successful presentation to the MAOGA members on our latest financial projections, as well as approval for the construction of the stadium. Frazier and I had worked long and hard at positioning the presentation in the best light by inviting individual media representatives for one-on-one briefings before he went to MAOGA. Our financial situation was always precarious, and the media remained suspicious of our rosy projections, so getting them on board was critical. Frazier was terrific in giving time he really couldn't spare to the *Wall Street Journal*, *Associated Press*, *Reuters*, the *New York Times*, and the *Atlanta Journal-Constitution*. He was forthright and responsive, and the media, both national and local, seemed impressed.

This same confidence was carried into the MAOGA board meeting. Once the meeting was over, all the questions answered and everyone was headed back to their offices in a state of elation, Billy Payne met me at the elevator for what I thought would be a "well done" but, instead, he jumped me about keeping him out of the process. I hadn't considered his involvement necessary. Again, his job as CEO was to focus on the big picture and leave the details to his chief operating officer. It had worked like a charm, but now I was being castigated because Payne had not had a role in the details.

My reaction was to quit on the spot. I would have walked out the door at that point except that I had a reporter in my office and needed to take care of his request first. As we finished, Payne called me to come see him.

Our offices were less than fifty feet apart. When I walked in, we had both cooled off. He suggested I cut back the hours I was working (I never did), that I get an assistant to help me (which I did), and reminded me in a gentle way that I was not working at BellSouth anymore and Olympic planning was never going to be neat and pretty, so I might as well get used to it (I tried). I was back in the office early the next morning as though nothing had happened. Clearly, I was shifting out of the corporate mode and into the Olympic environment.

A year-and-a-half later, I quit again when one of our contract guards asked to examine my briefcase as I left late one Friday. It seems that there had been some pilfering going on and maybe I looked guilty. Again, my ego got the best of me and my response was simply to hand my briefcase to the guard along with my ID badge and suggest he call upstairs and let them know that Dick Yarbrough wasn't coming back.

This time it was Frazier's turn to cool me off. He stopped by the house with my badge and my briefcase. We shared a libation or two; I apologized and was back at work on Monday. Two weeks later on a Friday, the tables were turned. Payne was conducting a meeting of the senior management along with Frazier and announced that any budget cuts proposed would have to be approved by him personally and there were some programs that he wasn't going to cut. No one quite knew the origin of that comment but smart money said one of the "insiders" had complained about having a program cut and Billy had reasserted his authority as CEO. Problem was, he should have told Frazier, not the rest of us.

Two weeks after giving me a pep talk, Frazier walks into Payne's office and turns in a "conditional letter of resignation." Payne took his discouraged friend to his lake home for the weekend and shared, I am sure, a few libations and the episode was soon forgotten. As the Games drew nearer, a fierce loyalty developed between Billy Payne and A. D. Frazier. Each appreciated, I think, the other's talents and forgot the encroachments into each other's territories.

Had any of the above incidents occurred at BellSouth or in any other corporate environment, business would have come to a grinding halt as people gathered around the water cooler and waxed breathlessly about the strange behavior of its senior management. At ACOG, nobody seemed to notice or, if they did, they didn't seem to care. Time spent discussing the doings of their temperamental managers was time better spent meeting a bunch of critical deadlines.

Gossip would just have to wait. The staff was too busy trying to get ready for the largest peacetime event in the twentieth century to worry about the fights and feuds among their leaders.

# 3

## BILLY PAYNE:
## IN A LEAGUE OF HIS OWN

If William Porter Payne were not real, you could not make him up. He is the most fascinating person I have ever known—and also the most complex. Unlike many people who exhibit one personality in public and another in private, with Billy Payne what you see is what you get.

I am often asked for my favorite Billy Payne story and there are too many to recount. One that does stand out occurred when President Clinton came to town in 1995 to address the ACOG employee body. Prior to the talk, the president was whisked into a holding room by the Secret Service and a few of us were invited in to shake hands and have our pictures taken with him. Once that was done, we simply stood around waiting to go downstairs to the auditorium where the employees were seated. The situation was a tad awkward. We were making small talk among ourselves, but how do you chitchat with the president of the United States? Billy solved that problem. Walking over to Bill Clinton, he asked, "How's your golf game?" The president recounted his most recent outing and averred as to how he had played better than usual that day. "I'd like to play with you sometime," said Payne. "I would like that very much," replied the president. Without hesitation, Billy said, "I'm gonna whup your ass." There was a moment's hesitation and then Clinton roared with laughter. It was vintage Payne. The honor of playing golf with the president of the United States was less important to him than beating him if he did. Did I say also that Billy Payne was the most competitive individual I have ever known?

Billy came by his competitive nature naturally. It was in his genes. His father, Porter Payne, had been an outstanding athlete in high school in Atlanta and had matriculated to the University of Georgia, where he had starred on some of the great Bulldog teams of the post-World War II era. He had been a tackle and had earned aAll-SEC honors in the process. When he was graduated in 1948, he was the first round draft choice of the New York Giants of the National Football League. In Billy's office at ACOG was a letter from Wellington Mara, owner of the Giants, offering Porter Payne the whopping sum of $10,000 to play professional football. For Billy's dad, it was a relatively easy decision to make. He went into the insurance business.

Porter Payne was an enormous influence on his son and as the father of two children myself, I can only hope that I may be as revered in their memory as Billy's dad is in his. Like his dad, Payne was an outstanding athlete. He was a high school quarterback, but people who knew him felt he was a Major League prospect as a baseball player.

In the meantime, the University of Georgia's football fortunes had waned considerably from the halcyon days of the late 1940's when the Bulldogs were a national power. During the 1950's, the Bulldogs barely broke even—winning fifty-one games and losing forty-nine—and limped into the 1960's as a perennial loser. In 1964, a young unknown assistant football coach from archrival Auburn University was hired to turn things around at UGA and the collective moan of the football faithful could be heard all over the state. His name was Vince Dooley and while not a popular choice at the time of his selection, he would win 201 football games, go to twenty bowls, and bring a national championship to Georgia before retiring in 1988 to become athletic director. He was also a powerful influence in the life of Billy Payne and remains so today.

One of Dooley's first innovations when arriving at the University of Georgia was to recruit quarterbacks to the team. Today, football is so specialized that kids begin their careers in Peewee Leagues as defensive backs or kickers or running backs, but in the 60's, the best athlete was always the quarterback. Most likely, he could play any position on the field but his teammates were less likely to be able to play his. Therefore, Dooley reasoned, I will recruit the best athletes available and put them at other positions when I get them here. His earliest recruiting classes included as many as seven quarterbacks who ended up in new roles at UGA. One of these was the quarterback from Dykes High School in Atlanta, Billy Payne.

People who know Payne as well as I do can't believe he actually considered going to school somewhere else, but he did. For a brief time, he thought of both Florida and Auburn, two of Georgia's most hated rivals, but Coach Dooley prevailed by holding out the promise of his playing baseball as well as football. At UGA, he was switched to end and he never played baseball thereafter. Dooley had recruited outstanding athletes and was building a very talented football team. If Billy Payne wanted to be on the first team, which was very important to him, baseball would have to give way to football. He would have to give it everything he had. He takes great pride, even today, of starting in every football game he played at Georgia. He had one close call. He remembers one week at practice when he got an inkling from an assistant coach that he might not start on Saturday. He was so panic-stricken at the thought that he went to the head coach to plead his case. It was another case of Payne's competitiveness. He had to start. It isn't enough to play. You have to be a starter. Dooley was so impressed with his intensity that he agreed. While at Georgia, Billy never played on the losing side in Sanford Stadium. In that period, the Bulldogs lost four games and played in three major bowls and won the SEC championship in 1968. He was a high achiever among a team of achievers, making all-SEC.

This brings to mind another favorite Billy Payne story. In 1995, he was selected an honorary coach for the spring G-Day Game, an inter-squad affair that signals the end of spring practice. His opponent was former Georgia governor and one-time UGA quarterback, Carl Sanders. The main purpose of the G-Day game is to excite the fans, run through some drills and avoid getting anyone hurt before the upcoming season— nothing serious, more of an exhibition than a real game. At halftime with his squad losing to Governor Sanders's team, Billy could stand it no longer. He assembled his squad on the sideline and read them the riot act. Visibly upset, Payne told them he had never lost a game at Sanford Stadium, and he wasn't going to lose one today. His shocked squad heard the message loud and clear and won the otherwise meaningless game. It didn't matter, by the way, that Governor Sanders was an influential member of the ACOG board of directors. Billy Payne was not going to lose to him or anybody else if he could help it.

His biggest competition has always been with himself. Rarely have I ever seen him satisfied with anything he has done. It goes back to his father. He has told the story many times of finishing a football game and asking his dad how he thought he had done. Invariably, Porter Payne's reply was "How do you think you did, Billy? Do you think you really did your best?" Billy could never say, "Yes, I did," because he could remember one play or maybe two that he could have done better and would vow to improve the next week. I found it interesting in talking to Billy about his days on the football field that on the night before the big game (and Georgia had a lot of big games in those days), he would sleep like a baby when his teammates were too excited or nervous to sleep. Yet, after the game was over, everyone else could relax and sleep but that was when Payne stayed awake all night, replaying the game in his mind and thinking of where he could have been better.

His drive for excellence carried over into the classroom at the University of Georgia. He was an outstanding student and served as vice president of the student body. He also made the best decision of his life while in college. He decided to marry the only girl he dated at Georgia, Martha Beard, of Moultrie, Georgia. It was as if stabilizers had been attached to a rocket. This lovely, levelheaded, kind woman has given Billy Payne two children, Elizabeth and Porter, and a great marriage. It may be the only thing he has ever done in his life that Payne can admit he could not have done better.

Following graduation he spurned the possibility of pro football even though the pay was better than when his dad had finished. Billy was accepted to the UGA law school and finished in the top one-fifth of his class in 1973.

After practicing in a law firm, Payne decided to branch out on his own with friend and college law school colleague Read Morton, specializing in real estate law. Even though the real estate market was soft in Atlanta, the firm prospered. He worked with the same drive that he had exhibited on the football field, excelling in the business world.

Then his personal world came crashing down. In 1983, Porter Payne died of a heart attack at the age of fifty-three. Billy had lost his idol.

Beyond a burning desire to succeed, Billy Payne had inherited something else from his dad—heart problems. Ironically, just five weeks after his father's death, Payne underwent triple bypass surgery. At age thirty-four life suddenly didn't look as simple as it had: work hard, achieve success; work harder, achieve more success. There had to be something more.

A couple of years later, Billy Payne experienced a seminal moment that changed his life forever and turned his city upside down in the process. He volunteered to head a capital funds drive for his church. What followed is a story that is too hokey to be believed. But it is true and even if you have heard it before, it bears repeating.

St. Luke's Presbyterian Church in suburban Dunwoody asked Billy to chair a campaign to raise $2.5 million for a new sanctuary. As would be expected, he was successful, and he basked in his accomplishment at the dedication of the sanctuary in February 1987. It was a great feeling. Instead of driving himself toward a personal goal, he had persuaded others toward a common goal, and in doing so had done something good for a larger community—his church.

On the way home, he told Martha what a wonderful feeling that was and that it was something he wanted to experience again. Little did she know where that was heading.

The next morning at 4:00 AM in his law office, he took out a legal pad and wrote down some ideas that he thought worth pursuing. Super Bowl. Political conventions. In Billy's mind, all were too ordinary. Only one item he had written down seemed big enough: "An Olympics." Atlanta had made a feeble attempt a few years earlier to investigate the possibility of Olympic Games but nothing had come of it. This time it would be different. He would bring the Olympics to Atlanta.

There were a couple of problems. He didn't know when the next Games were scheduled, how one went about securing the Olympic Games, or who the International Olympic Committee was. No big deal. All that information he found in the library. The next Olympic Games to be awarded would be for 1996, the centennial anniversary of the modern Olympics. Anyone who knew anything about the Olympic Movement knew that Athens, Greece, would host them as they had the 1896 Games. That was a lock.

Unaware of that information, Billy announced to Martha his plan to bring the Olympic Games to Atlanta. As Payne has told the story many times, Martha knew better than to tell him such a dream was an impossibility. Rather, she suggested that he call his good friend, Peter Candler, the most conservative, cautious man she knew. She felt sure he would give the idea a good splash of cold water and everyone could get on with their lives. Billy called Candler told him that he wanted to recruit a small group of people capable of writing $50,000 checks and go after the 1996 Games. To Martha Payne's astonishment, Candler said, "Why not?" The impossible dream was underway.

It was then that Ginger Watkins and Linda Stephenson joined the team, followed by Horace Sibley of King & Spalding, and a member of one of the Atlanta's most prominent families. After Sibley came Charlie Battle, Charlie Schaffer, Tim Christian, Cindy Fowler, and Bobby Reardon. The team was in place.

You can have big dreams and be willing to work hard to achieve those dreams, but you also need some good fortune, as well. That was the case with the team that Payne had assembled. Before any effort could be made to involve Atlanta in such an effort as the Olympic Games, it would need the sanction of the city. Sibley arranged for Billy Payne to meet with the mayor of Atlanta, Andrew Young. Young, in his second term as mayor and ineligible to run again, sensed Payne's sincerity and gave the idea his blessing. The former ambassador to the United Nations and one of the Third World's most beloved figures gave the effort instant credibility. There is no question that any other mayor would have balked at the idea, established conditions too onerous to be practical (like racial quotas), or would have given it lip service. Andy Young did none of the above and, once out of office, was a major player in the bid efforts. At the time Young was mayor, Bob Holder, chairman of Holder Construction and one of Atlanta's most prominent businessmen, was president of the Atlanta Chamber of Commerce. Another stroke of good timing. Just as Andy Young brought credibility in the international arena, Holder gave Billy Payne and his team credibility with the business community. That would enable the group to raise the big money necessary to pursue their dream. I don't know if another chamber president would have had the standing among his peers that Bob Holder did. Everything was clicking.

But not everybody was convinced of the worth of the idea.

At a BellSouth officers meeting at Callaway Gardens, one of our attorneys, Vin Sgrosso, mentioned to our vice chairman, John White, and me that some lawyers from King & Spalding wanted to bring Billy Payne by to talk about our helping them with an Olympic tape they wanted to do in order to bid for the Olympic Games. White said okay, and I set the meeting up for the next week.

We listened as Billy, Charlie Battle, and Charlie Schaffer told us that Atlanta was going after the 1996 Games but before they could do that, they must obtain the endorsement of the United States Olympic

Committee. No city could bid without the sanction of their national Olympic organization. Several other US cities were also in the running for 1996. They were looking for $25,000. White heard their story and agreed to the request.

Much later, when Atlanta had been awarded the Games in Tokyo, Billy Payne was a hero. He returned home to a welcome unseen since the premier of *Gone with the Wind* some fifty years earlier. One of Payne's first trips upon his arrival was to Athens to see his Bulldogs play football. Each Saturday before a home game, the president of the university hosts a luncheon at his home for selected alumni, faculty, and political figures. It had been my good fortune to attend a number of the luncheons, including the day Billy showed up to the adulation of the assembled guests. At that time, Payne and I did not know each other well. I am ten years older and our paths had not crossed at UGA or anywhere else for that matter. As Billy was accepting congratulations on his achievement, he pointed to me and said, "There is the real hero." I was stunned and had no idea what he was talking about. He went on, "When no one in town would see us or return our calls, we went to BellSouth and they gave us the money for a videotape. It was the first time we didn't have to dig into our own pockets." That made me the center of attention in the room. How could this guy have been so prescient? What did he know then that we didn't know? I quickly brought the crowd back to reality.

"Billy," I said, "I must tell you what I told John White when you left that day." With that, I could sense everybody wanted to know what I had said. It had to be very wise, no doubt.

"I looked at John and said, 'Well, you can kiss that $25,000 goodbye.'" So much for prescience.

I was not a part of the bid committee or the thousands of volunteers it attracted. I did not experience first-hand what went on in those years prior to 1990. I was too busy dealing with BellSouth's issues to worry about what Billy Payne was doing.

For someone who had no experience in the international world of Olympic politics, Payne's plan was extraordinarily simple. He knew that the vote by the IOC members would be done in secret. That meant they didn't have to explain their votes to anyone. He decided to make the members like the Atlanta team better than they liked any of the other bid city teams. For those who might object to the Olympic Games coming back to the United States so soon after Los Angeles, the Atlantans sought to assure the IOC that Atlanta was so far away from LA as to be almost in another part of the world—an argument on which both Atlantans and the people of Los Angeles would be in complete agreement.

For a man who had never been out of the country, Payne lost count of the number of countries he visited but thinks it more than 105. The team of ten original volunteers traveled the globe, meeting IOC members and heaping on loads of Southern charm. As members of the Olympic family came to Atlanta, they were feted by the locals and treated like royalty (which they feel they are). They went to football games at the University of Georgia and at Georgia Tech. They played golf at Augusta. They came to the BellSouth Classic golf tournament, with which I had some involvement. They shot quail on South Georgia plantations.

Gushing along with the volunteers was the local newspaper, which reported on all the details of the bid effort. There was little, if anything, they didn't know. After all, it was in their economic interest to have the Olympic Games in Atlanta. It would give them some much needed respectability among their peers in the media and would ensure a lot of advertising opportunities. After the Games, Payne refused to open up bid information when requested by the paper—the organization was a private group as defined by law and not required to do so—the howls of righteous indignation were immediate and threatening. What they wanted to see they already knew. They just didn't like being told "no."

At the same time that the Atlantans were pulling out all the stops and beginning to make some headway with the members, Athens was shooting itself in the foot with an arrogance that matched the IOC's. The Greeks are wonderful, warm people. They also are very emotional about the Olympics. It is their strong view that the Olympics are theirs, no matter where the IOC might be located. To use as simple an explanation as I can, they thought them up. Thousands of years ago, warring cities would put down their weapons for a few days and engage in a peaceful competition in Olympia. That was several eons before Coca-Cola ever dreamed of becoming a major sponsor.

So the Athens bid team was having a hard time intellectually understanding why they had to beg for what was theirs, just as a group of wide-eyed idealists from Atlanta was putting its own efforts into overdrive. It was beginning to dawn on Payne and the others that they just might have a chance to pull this miracle off.

On September 20, 1990 in the city of Tokyo, IOC president Juan Antonio Samaranch uttered the historic words that brought Billy Payne's dream to fruition, "The International Olympic Committee has awarded the 1996 Olympic Games to the city of...AHT-lanta." The ten volunteers who had anted up $50,000 apiece in pursuit of the Olympic Games had done the impossible.

As the announcement was being made in Tokyo, I was in Orlando, Florida, hosting a meeting of the Arthur Page Society, an organization of top corporate public relations officers from around the country. I am a stickler for starting meetings on time but this one would have to be delayed until I could see the announcement, which was being televised. When I heard Samaranch's words, I walked onto the stage, greeted everyone and told the assembly that Jane and I were inviting them all — there were about 200 in the room — to our house in 1996. Atlanta had just won the Olympic Games. And it all began when Billy was asked to raise money to build a new church sanctuary.

As you would expect, William Porter Payne returned from Tokyo to great acclaim. He had pulled off the greatest upset in Olympics history and had given his hometown a gift beyond comprehension. Imagine, the world was coming to Atlanta in six short years. The city would be front page news around the world. It is the kind of situation chambers of commerce can only dream about; yet in Atlanta, it was reality. And reality was about to sink in.

In Tokyo, a host city contract was signed and the bidding committee was dissolved. A new organization had to be set up to organize the Games. Would the members of the bid committee, including Payne, be selected to operate them as well?

Andrew Young was no longer mayor. Maynard Jackson was. When Andy Young talks about the civil rights movement, it isn't some abstract conversation. He was there on the front lines as Dr. Martin Luther King, Jr.'s top lieutenant. He had endured beatings, threats, and slurs that those of us who are white can only imagine. Yet, he came through those difficult times as a kind and forgiving man. If love is a weapon in the human rights struggle, Andy is the chief warrior. It was because of people like him and Dr. King that blacks finally got their deserved place at the economic table. Some of those who did get there, however, could be accused of wanting second-helpings before anybody else had a chance to see the plate passed the first time.

Maynard Jackson, who in the early '70s had become Atlanta's first minority mayor, had broken the hold of white political power brokers on city government. He had been succeeded by Andy Young after two terms as mayor and was now in turn succeeding Young. Jackson had a huge ego. Where Young was quiet and thoughtful, Jackson was outspoken and forceful, even a little intimidating. To be kind, being on a world stage was not something that he dreaded. He would enjoy the spotlight.

Jackson also wanted a larger role in the organization of the Games, and Payne was vulnerable. The business community had wondered if a real estate attorney with little management experience was really up to the task of managing something as complicated as the Olympic Games and had even entertained the idea of bringing Peter Ueberroth, the architect of the successful Los Angeles Games, to Atlanta. In my opinion, there wasn't a corporate CEO in town who could have withstood the uncertainties of organizing the Games.

Also, the mayor had not been a part of the bid committee and had not had much to do with the process. The bid document didn't plan for any help from the city government to raise money and to build the facilities. That was going to be done with private dollars. Jackson expressed concern about hiring practices, i.e., minority participation. He demanded veto power over Olympic operating plans in general and the $500 million construction program in particular. But he had found his match in Billy Payne.

With the business community's endorsement and the backing of the International Olympic Committee, Billy was set to do battle with Maynard Jackson over the one thing that both men share in common—the need for control. The mayor wanted it in order to have some say over what was built in his city and where and by whom. Jackson managed to wring some compromises from Payne but not enough to have any significant control over the planning process.

Billy wanted it because he was not willing to entrust his dream to anyone else. Somewhere along the way in trying to achieve his big idea scratched out on the yellow note pad just a few years earlier, Billy Payne had caught the Olympic spirit.

This was to be both his strength and his blind spot. Because he is so bright, Billy grew enormously in the job as CEO of the Atlanta Committee for the Olympic Games. He learned reluctantly the necessity to delegate because the type of people he attracted to the Games neither wanted nor needed much direction. He learned to make the thousands of little compromises one must make to get things accomplished. He even learned to accept the criticism that comes with being in charge of something as visible as the Olympic Games (Although he never liked it, particularly if it upset Martha). But one thing that he never accepted was any individual or any group who put their own interests ahead of the goodness of the Olympic spirit. Sometimes I think he was an idealist; other times, I think he was the only person in the Olympic movement that really understood what the Games were all about. He could never intellectually come to terms with the fact that the Olympic Games provided special interest groups a world-wide megaphone to espouse their cause—groups that didn't give a damn if the Games were held or not, just as long as they could make their views known to the world.

Suddenly, some of the folks who had been throwing confetti on Payne were now hurling brickbats—the unions, the inner city neighborhoods and their allies, the preachers, politicians, environmentalists, the disabled, pro-state flag, anti-state flag. The list was endless. I used to say to my colleagues that we would have to extend the Atlanta Games another month if we were to get all the protesters their 15 minutes of fame. There seemed that many.

Billy's initial reaction was to take them on. It was his football mentality. I would kid him later that I wish he had been a wide receiver in college—a position with finesse. Defensive ends are trained to lower their heads, plow through three or four blockers, find the ball carrier and put him on his tail. That is a wonderful trait on the football field but it doesn't necessarily carry over to running an organization like ACOG. Sometimes, you have got to use some finesse.

It was one such incident that got me to the Atlanta Committee—golf at Augusta. It seems Billy Payne wasn't through making miracles. Having secured the Games for Atlanta, Billy had talked the International Olympic Committee into adding golf. There are some sports that have been pleading for inclusion in the Olympic Games for years with no success. Payne had convinced the IOC to add golf to the 1996 Games. Incredibly, Augusta National Golf Club agreed to host the venue. Most golfers consider Augusta the most hallowed golfing spot in the country. It also was exclusively white and male. Billy's thinking was that golf would be a natural for television, increasing the value of broadcast rights. It would also open Augusta up to women and minorities. In short, there was something for everybody.

The result was a firestorm. Billy had not done his due diligence in the external environment. He failed to reach out to black politicians in Atlanta who considered Augusta National racist. He gave them a sitting duck for a target. Led by then city council member Bill Campbell, who was to follow Maynard Jackson as mayor of Atlanta, the council raised holy hell, issuing a "non-binding" resolution against the move.

Bob Holder had seen enough. He wanted someone who had some experience in the external environment and a temperament that could stand up to Payne's personality and keep Billy from being such a lightning rod for controversy. That is how I ended up at the Atlanta Committee for the Olympic Games.

I had developed a reputation for being able to "manage" strong CEOs, and John Clendenin was one of the strongest. Public relations done well is no different that an attorney's job. Both give counsel. One gives it in the external environment, the other in the legal environment. Sometimes an organization can be within safe boundaries legally and still lose badly in the court of public opinion. Despite that fact, most top managers have almost no understanding of how complex the external world is. It is made up of a number of publics, all of whom have varying degrees of influence in how the organization operates. I call them stakeholders. Most companies, including BellSouth, don't like to be reminded of that. It interferes with the neat five-year business plans.

Despite the fact that most corporate executives don't have a clue about how the external environment works, I never recall in thirty-five years in the business anybody admitting that. Everybody is a public relations expert.

While these executives will show proper deference to their attorneys (I say it is because the lawyers resort to speaking Latin when they feel they might not get their way. The only Latin I know is "E Pluribus Unum" and that never won me a battle with the lawyers.), they will underestimate the power of the outside world and become very direct in what they expect from their public relations counsel—i.e., "get good stuff in the paper and keep the bad stuff out."

While I am sermonizing, let me say that the reason corporations pay lip service to the public relations discipline is that those of us who practice it don't do a very good job. It is no fun confronting your boss or your peers and telling them that what is being planned won't work because, in your opinion, the external environment won't accept it. You can get unpopular in a hurry with your management.

You also work under a cloud of suspicion. The media are a conduit to reach those publics who can impact an organization and you need to keep the lines of communications open to get to them. The media are also a favorite target of corporate management who ascribe — sometimes correctly — a bias to their coverage. Usually, however, it isn't bias. It is that the reporter can't possibly know everything about the business that management knows, and must also take pains to get the other side of a story. The result is a story that management doesn't like and one they believe could have been better had their PR people done a better job. On the other hand, the media views their public relations contact as duplicitous, not forthcoming, and in short, a company shill. Therefore, many PR types choose to go along and get along. They figure they will live longer that way.

Also, your mistakes are hard to hide. If the marketers or engineers make a mistake, the boss may or may not find out about it. When your public relations person goofs — as I have done many times — you and your boss can read about it in the newspaper or watch it on television at the same time.

Despite that and despite the fact that I had never taken a public relations course in college, I had enjoyed some success and notoriety as an influential public relations practitioner in a large corporation with a good reputation. That I could be adversarial in defending the external environment would be a plus.

I learned something early on about Billy Payne that is, to my mind, his most important strength. Unlike most people I have worked with over the years — and maybe I should include myself in the mix — Billy knows what he doesn't know and never fakes it. That is the sign of a very confident individual. Watching him work a crowd or talking to the president of the United States, you would never know that he had little interest in the complexities of the external world. Unlike most corporate executives, however, he would freely admit that and ask for my help in walking through the political and special interest minefields before him. He would question and he would argue but in the end, if the advice made sense, he would follow it. He was consistent in not agreeing to interviews or speeches without first discussing it. Even in my best days at BellSouth, I had not had this kind of relationship with my boss. Some of my fondest memories are of our 6:30 AM meetings when we would talk strategy, football, and share our personal feelings with each other.

Something unusual happened to me in the process. I had been trained throughout my career to support the institution that employed me. I could criticize it internally, question its operational decisions and bring back inside the feedback of the stakeholders as a means of changing those decisions, but as the first line of defense to the outside world, I was expected to defend my company vigorously and I could. Who was making those decisions was not as important as the results. Managers in a corporation come and go. The organization remains. ACOG was the exact opposite. The group would be around along long enough to put on the Games and then it would be gone. Who was running it was of paramount importance.

I never quite caught the Olympic spirit to the extent that Billy, Charlie Battle, Ginger Watkins, Linda Stephenson, and the original group of ten had. I was a hired gun, an "outsider." I found much of the pomp and circumstance ridiculous and many of the IOC members irrelevant. I could count on the fingers of one hand the ones who could have even gotten an appointment with my chief executive officer at BellSouth, John Clendenin. But then I hadn't been around at the outset of the effort, either. Maybe if I had, I would have had more loyalty to the Olympic movement.

But I hadn't been there long before I developed a fierce loyalty to Billy Payne. I saw what he was doing as ennobling and self-sacrificing. Because of his own enthusiasm, he was a target of ridicule from the local newspaper who had taken his belief that ACOG was staging "the greatest peacetime event of the twentieth century" and equated it with Barnum's "Greatest Show on Earth." His detractors, including the media, attacked him as racist, homophobic, arrogant, rich, and irrelevant to the planning of the Games.

Soon after I arrived, Billy had his second triple bypass in April 1993. There was no question that the strain was getting to him. He was trying to do the right thing for a city that seemed more interested in making money off of his efforts than in supporting him. I became defensive of him and in doing so, lost a little of the outside perspective I was required to bring to the job.

It seemed to please Billy to have someone who was as intense as he was on the team. At the time I interviewed with him for the job, it was clear he really wasn't that excited about the deal. For one thing, it would mean moving some responsibility from his close friend Ginger Watkins who had public relations in her department. Billy decided to test me. "You need to understand that I am the most intense individual you will ever know," he said. I shot back, "Yeah, and I am in the top three." He liked that response.

Soon after Sydney won the rights for the 2000 Games, the then-CEO of that organization was walking with Billy up the stairs from a dinner in Monaco, seeking advice. I was walking behind them. "The first thing you want to do," Billy opined and nodded in my direction, "is to get you a mean son-of-a-bitch like him." I thought that a very nice compliment.

My protectiveness showed in other ways, too, particularly with the Secret Service. We walked a balancing act for most of the time before and during the Games. We welcomed the interest of the Clinton Administration because it gave us some leverage in getting the kind of government support we needed. A part of that involvement was the frequent appearance of the president or First Lady or the vice president or Mrs. Gore. Inevitably, when they came, so came a throng of Secret Service agents. There is no question that protecting the lives of our leaders is more important than the Olympic Games, but at the same time, the Secret Service could be guilty of absurd overkill (Pardon the pun). Ginger Watkins had just about taken their heads off on several occasions when they arbitrarily changed some of her plans as related to opening or closing ceremonies. Ginger was understandably irate and let them know, while at the same time changing things back to the way they were originally. I had my own problems with them and all of them, but one related to Billy Payne.

Somewhere in Secret Service training, there must have been a module on blankness. When you get in their face, they develop this blank stare and rigid position. All that seems to be missing is repeating a mantra or humming loud enough to drown out the words. When the torch arrived in Los Angeles from overseas, we had a massive celebration there. We had gotten word that Tipper Gore wanted to be a part of the festivities. No one at ACOG was jumping up and down about it but since we had Governor Miller representing the state, why not?

The ceremony was impressive and emotional. We finally had the Olympic flame on US soil and it was about to start the trip across the country to Atlanta. Once the ceremony was over, I had Billy set to go back up on stage to meet with the media. The only problem was that a secret service agent with the ubiquitous earplug and dark glasses was blocking the way. It was Billy's show and he couldn't even get on the stage because Tipper Gore, who had invited herself, was still there. This wasn't pre-planned. It was just the way they seemed to work. I went a little berserk and found myself being calmed down by Billy, rather than the other way around. As always, I complained and, as always, I received assurances it wouldn't happen again. But there would be other times where they intruded on our Games unnecessarily. The most flagrant was opening ceremonies. When President Clinton went down to the field to await the official ceremonies, the Secret Service agent inexplicably turned off the elevator leaving Payne and Samaranch to bolt down the steps in order to kick off the 1996 Games. Clinton was the guest, but the hosts were having trouble getting to their own party.

We managed to avoid a problem with them at the lighting of the Flame in Olympia. I had an idea that the Secret Service would be swarming all over the place since Mrs. Clinton and Chelsea were in attendance. This was one of the big days in Billy's life, so while he and the others paced the grounds reflectively, I sought out the Secret Service agent in charge of the First Lady's contingent. With chutzpah I didn't know I had, I boldly told him that this was Billy Payne's big day and I didn't want him or his agents mucking it up. I didn't even want Payne to see them. If Billy was walking somewhere, then it was up to them to see that he got there without interference. I must have been earnest. The agent in charge chuckled and said, "Don't worry, I hear you loud and clear." There was no problem that day. In fact, it was a great day all around. I don't know if Billy ever heard how his "mean son-of-a-bitch" intervened on his behalf, but I doubt he would be surprised.

I see Billy occasionally now; usually at a meeting of the University of Georgia, where we both serve as Foundation trustees. I remain as loyal to him today as I did when I was a part of his big dream. Following the Games, he should have received the keys to the city from City Hall and a dinner from the Chamber of Commerce. He got neither. He folded up his tent and went to NationsBank as vice chairman. Subsequent to that, he joined Premiere Technologies in Atlanta and is president of one of its subsidiaries and a member of several corporate boards. He has also been chastised by the local newspaper for his insistence that his private records were his. It has been a big yawn to the majority of Atlantans. It heartens me that the general public has the same view of him that I do. He is a bona fide hero.

We will never see his like again.

# 4

## FINANCING THE GAMES: HIGH RISK, NO NET

When Billy Payne and friends won the opportunity to host the 1996 Centennial Games in Atlanta, he introduced a new Olympic sport to the city—Financial Tightrope Walking. This unique competition consisted of the Atlanta Committee for the Olympic Games attempting to raise large sums of money from the private sector and having no safety net (translation: government backing) to catch us if we fell. This high wire act was made even more perilous by the countervailing forces pulling at us as we attempted to maneuver our way to financial safety. On one side were the citizens of Atlanta, who had cheered mightily when Payne pulled off his miracle, but despite constant assurances to the contrary, were developing a major case of angst about their taxes going up because the Olympic Games were being held in Atlanta. Never mind that the city was indemnified by contract from the costs of putting on the games. Never mind that the event would have an economic impact of over $5 billion in the state, including $100-200 million in increased tax revenues. Never mind that we were turning over more than $400 million in new construction projects to various governmental and educational entities at the end of the Games. Never mind that we were developing a new twenty-one acre park for the city in the heart of a blighted downtown area. Never mind that we had relieved the city of $11 million of debt on the old baseball stadium and were giving them a new one valued at $209 million to keep the Atlanta Braves from leaving downtown. Many people couldn't be convinced that the city wasn't going to become another Montreal, where in 1976, the Olympic Games left that city a legacy of a one billion dollar debt.

How concerned were people? When my wife's uncle died shortly before the Games, we paid our respects to the family at a small funeral home just south of the city. A cousin introduced me to friends of the late uncle who began immediately to berate me — a perfect stranger — in front of the group, because in their opinion the Games were going to bankrupt the state and raise their taxes beyond their means. I was startled at their ignorance and bad taste, but that night was just another reminder that the Centennial Olympic Games were too big for many of our locals, not physically, but psychologically.

Wringing their hands on the other side were members of the International Olympic Committee, who had succumbed to the persuasive charms of Payne and his volunteer army and had awarded to Atlanta their prize possession, the celebration of the centennial anniversary of the modern Olympic Games. The IOC considered the Games their "franchise" to be "loaned out" every four years and they expected that the event would be returned to them in as good, or better, shape as it had been when it left Lausanne. They had a different problem. What they saw once the planning began was an enterprise that made them very uncomfortable. There were obviously going to be no government guarantees and there were certainly no guarantees that the private sector — American corporations — would be willing to pay some ten times what a sponsorship had cost in Los Angeles in 1984. All they had to go on was Payne's unshakeable faith that we would succeed.

The IOC's concern wasn't the potential liability for the taxpayers of Georgia. They feared if we didn't get all the money required, we would have to cut the quality of the Games, not to mention a few thousand creature comforts that the Olympic aristocracy deemed their divine right. Riding in an Atlanta cab instead of their usual limousine was as odious to the IOC as the possibility of raising taxes was to the citizens of Atlanta.

Watching this precarious balancing act were the local and national media and our financial watchdog, the steely-eyed Metropolitan Atlanta Olympic Games Authority (MAOGA). Reports of a lack of financial progress came early in the planning process and were with us to the end. I have often suspected that most members of the media can't balance their own checkbooks, even with the meager amount their organizations pay them. I know for a fact that the study of business principles is as rare in our journalism schools as the abacus is in accounting classes. Yet, like caterpillars that become butterflies, reporters magically develop into fiscal experts when the subject is somebody else's money. That allowed them to feed the public's (and the IOC's) doubts about our fiscal abilities.

As early as December 1992—three years and seven months before the Games were scheduled to begin—the *Atlanta Journal-Constitution* ran a front-page story about the lack of progress of our marketing efforts to date. As the paper ominously reported, "only" four companies had signed up for the $40 million sponsorships. I was still at BellSouth wrapping up my old job when I read this. My first thought was four $40 million sponsors this far ahead of the Games sounded impressive. Also, I wasn't sure that the reporter understood how complicated high-level business negotiations could be.

Early on, ACOG had agreed to make public on a quarterly basis records that included financial reports (after we had shown them to MAOGA), the key terms of television contracts we had signed and a list of sponsors, once we had them signed. We would tell neither MAOGA nor the media what kind of deal we had made with a sponsor because of the impact that might have on future negotiations with future sponsors. The question was always, how much to tell the media so that they can get a clear picture of where we are financially and yet not reveal enough details of our sponsorships so that we tipped off a potential sponsor on how much another had paid. It was a fine line we walked through the entire planning process.

There was nothing else to do but raise the money—lots of it. Putting on the Centennial Olympic Games in Atlanta was going to cost an estimated $1.7 billion. The plan in 1993 was to get 41% through our and the IOC's marketing efforts, 35% from the sale of broadcast rights fees around the world, 14% from ticket sales, 2% from merchandising and 8% from "all other"—donations, concession and program sales, rental of space and equipment to constituent groups (such as the press), interest income, sale of assets etc.

To sell the sponsorships, the Atlanta Committee for the Olympic Games entered into a joint venture with the United States Olympic Committee, creating an organization known as Atlanta Centennial Olympic Properties (ACOP). The venture was established to avoid conflicts in two separate marketing efforts by two separate Olympic organizations to one set of sponsors. Why not sell together? Those who paid the estimated $40 million would come as Centennial Olympic

Partners, with access to choice hotel rooms, preferred parking, hospitality opportunities, and broader access to various venues, they would receive an attractive ticket package, but not just the premium events; they had to buy tickets to some of the lesser-known sports, as well. In addition, ACOP worked with the IOC on marketing international sponsorships. This program was known as TOP (The Olympic Programme III) for companies seeking exposure in the international marketplace.

When the dust settled, the TOP program had ten sponsors, the joint venture had nine, and a smaller sponsorship program with limited rights and benefits had attracted twenty-four sponsors. Beyond that, a number of companies were identified as suppliers. That was not a misnomer, for they supplied us with a number of needed items from food to sports equipment to printing materials. Finally, there were the licensees who were sanctioned to produce everything from clothing apparel to Olympic pins.

First out of the box was NationsBank, now Bank of America. Hugh McColl, the dynamic chairman of the Charlotte, North Carolina-based company, was already making plans to become a national financial institution. The Atlanta Games could not have been timed better to give his bank that kind of exposure. A part of our negotiation with NationsBank included establishing a $300 million line of credit that we could draw on until money began coming into the coffers from other sources. Thanks to good financial management, we used less than a third the available line of credit.

After NationsBank, the deals became tougher to make. There were interminable meetings, negotiations, sticking points, etc. Not so with McColl. He knew what he wanted to do and did it. It is easy to understand why he now runs one of the largest financial institutions in the country.

For their money, sponsors received for the first time a well-coordinated effort to help protect them from ambushers, companies who swarm Olympic Games like flies, trying to piggyback on the high profile and basic positive feelings surrounding the Games without paying the fees. ACOP adopted a "take no prisoners" attitude toward potential ambushers, and in my view, kept what had been a perennial problem well managed.

A different problem emerged, however. With the number of partners, sponsors, and suppliers, there is the inevitable overlap of goods and services. Today's companies are very diverse, with a host of products and services to offer to the public. It seemed to be a law of physics that the smaller the sponsor/supplier, the more aggressive the effort to promote their association with the Atlanta Games.

One of our biggest headaches was the McDonalds' sponsorship. It was a Centennial Olympic Partner and its category was fairly obvious — food. At the same time, we made a deal with Aramark, an aggressive food supply company out of Philadelphia, to supply meals for the athletes. Aramark had developed a full-scale marketing effort with ads and news releases to take maximum advantage of their association with the Olympic Games, telling the world they were supplying food for the athletes. McDonald's, using their leverage with the USOC and with us, was raising hell because they considered Aramark as poaching on their territory.

ACOP personnel were aghast at the efforts of Aramark to position themselves like an Olympic sponsor and forbade such a program. On the other hand, the Olympic Village, which had the responsibility for feeding the athletes, didn't want Aramark offended. They were a critical supplier. Caught in the middle was Scott Mall, a member of my staff, who worked with all of the sponsors to help them get the most public bang for their buck. He was the one constant in the disagreement. All sides blamed him. So, Scott and I did what we always did in situations like this. We postured, cajoled, held innumerable meetings with the attorneys, and hoped that if we did all of the above long enough, the problem would go away in the euphoria of the Games. We did and it did.

About the closest thing to an ambush occurred when the United States Postal Service, an Olympics sponsor in 1992 but not in 1996, created a series of Olympic stamps as a part of the broader philatelic program encouraged by the IOC and decided to imprint the stamps on T-shirts and sell the shirts as a part of their own marketing program. We said that was not permitted. The USPS said it was their stamps and their T-shirts. While the marketers and the lawyers were circling each other like snarling dogs, it so happened that a good friend, Larry Speakes, was the USPS senior vice president in charge of external relations. Speakes, a former press secretary to President Ronald Reagan, didn't want a public fight and potential lawsuit any more than I did. We conferred privately, and plotted a strategy to inflict as little damage on each other's organization as possible. In the end, the Postal Service decided to drop the idea and a lot of time and money was saved by both sides.

After the Games were over, I was invited by Speakes to address a postal advisory committee meeting in Washington. Following my talk and with much flourish, he gave me a special gift of thanks—a set of T-shirts with Olympic stamps imprinted on them. I counted this one of my prized possessions until Speakes informed me that he had a warehouse full of them.

My biggest criticism of the marketing effort wasn't the zeal with which we went after and signed sponsors to participate in the Games, it was what the sponsors did with their investment. Typically, Billy Payne, ACOP president Bill McCahan, or USOC marketing chief John Krimsky made a sponsorship deal with a corporation's top management, usually the CEO. That was logical because a sponsorship was big bucks, even for the biggest companies. In many cases once the deal was made, the companies would give the responsibility for administering the sponsorship to some mid-level manager with little authority to do anything substantive. Hopefully, they were carrying messages to and from top management but I'm not sure that most corporations received the maximum benefit from what they spent.

Despite all the trials and tribulations, doubts and second-guessing, the end result was success. ACOP had set a record for raising revenues—some $672.5 million, including $573 million from sponsors and suppliers. Of that total, over $435.7 million went straight to ACOG's bottom line.

Another major source of revenue came from the sale of broadcast rights around the world. In its original plans, the committee had forecast some $549 million as our share of the worldwide TV revenue. We had received $175 million as our part of the European Broadcasting Union (EBU)'s record $250 million agreement and needed at least $379 million if we were to stay on budget. The biggest rights sale of them all would be in the United States. We would receive 60% of the total with the rest going to the International Olympic Committee. We were hoping for $500 million, which would put our share in the range of $290-$300 million and leave us "only" $80-$90 million to reach our target. But our timing wasn't very good.

Los Angeles television rights had gone for $225 million in 1984 to ABC. According to Los Angeles chief Peter Ueberroth in his book, *Made in America*, he had expected to get $200 million. His board had expected only half that. In the intervening years, the cost of rights fees for sports had gone up precipitously but not necessarily viewership. CBS had paid over a billion dollars to major league baseball for a four-year deal that was coming to a close and was reported to have lost $500,000. NBC had paid $401 million for the rights to the 1992 Games in Barcelona and had lost about $100 million, much of it due to an ill-fated effort to charge cable viewers for commercial-free coverage on three different cablecasts. Even four years after the Barcelona Games, some advertising agencies saw no increased value in the 1996 Games. Our point was that being in the Eastern time zone of the United States would give the winning network a huge base of viewers, plus the fact that it was the centennial anniversary of the modern Games. The IOC, which would act as lead negotiator, was suggesting a baseline number of $450 million to start the bidding. "Not a chance in hell," one ad executive told *USA Today*, "I don't think they'll get $401 million." A financial analyst told *Reuters* that "Olympic organizers could be hard-pressed to get much more than $400 million. At a point around $400 million, it stops making economic sense."

There was also speculation that Atlanta-based Turner Broadcasting would have a presence in the negotiations. Turner Network Television (TNT) had agreed to a partnership with CBS for the 1994 Winter Olympics. The Turner people promptly announced that not only would they not be interested in a partnership in their hometown, they would have to be paid to carry any part of the Atlanta Games. A Turner Network executive explained that their decision was due to the fact that they were not expecting to do well financially in their CBS Winter Olympics deal and were fully aware of how poorly NBC's cable venture had done earlier in Barcelona. I ascribe more ulterior motives to their decision.

When Billy Payne stunned Atlanta with his success in bringing the Olympic Games to Atlanta, it took the spotlight off of Ted Turner. Finally, there was somebody in Atlanta with more imagination and guts than Turner. The price for Billy's success was almost no cooperation from Turner or his organization. Look no further than the "business decision" not to support the Atlanta Games. Such business acumen did not extend to the money-hemorrhaging Goodwill Games, a Turner creation that started out as a competition between the US and the Soviet Union but now seems intent on being an Olympic Games wannabe.

Other than some small help financially on Centennial Olympic Park which is near the CNN Center, he did little else. That extended, of course, to his organization's insistence that they be paid to carry the Games.

Because so much money was involved, television negotiations were a high-profile event. We had spent much time strategizing before leaving for New York on Sunday evening, July 25. The meetings were being held in private offices in the Citicorp Building in midtown. Heading the negotiating time was Dick Pound, an attorney from Montreal and member of the IOC executive committee. With him were Francois Carrard, the director general of the IOC, and Dr. Un Yong Kim, another member of the executive board, from South Korea, site of the 1988 Games. With that group would be members of the USOC, more IOC staff members, and our group of a half dozen from Atlanta.

The IOC wanted us to delay negotiations because they thought the market would be stronger later in the year. But we couldn't because we had to have the money before MAOGA would agree to approve our stadium financing. Maybe we would have done better if we had waited, but it is a moot point today.

The trip got off to a rough start. Not knowing how the Atlanta papers would treat the event, I retrieved a first edition on Saturday evening. The story was on the front page, bottom left, with the headline that, "Payne to TV Networks: Let the Games Begin." Happily, the story wasn't negative, either. After three decades in the business, I should have known better. Sometime between the first edition and the Final Home edition, which goes to most of the subscribers, the story had been moved to the bottom right on the front page and had a new headline, "Games Success, Payne's Reputation Ride on TV Negotiations." A totally different headline with an editorial slant. Billy called me as upset as I could remember him, and I didn't blame him. I also couldn't explain why such a change in headlines. The best I could do was to surmise that someone in moving the story on the page had decided to put a new head on the story. But it had ratcheted up the pressure on us even more than ever and focused the public on our financial tightrope-walking act.

Our frustrations were just beginning. The team was housed in a hotel, that I shall let go nameless, was it terrible—too small, inadequate meeting rooms, and a facility for a press conference that might have served us well had we been announcing the seating arrangements for lunch. But this was about who would telecast the Centennial Olympic Games in Atlanta in 1996. This was big news. Bigger, unfortunately, than the hotel.

We gathered in the hotel's "penthouse" to discuss our strategies that consisted primarily of how much money we thought we would get and how that number would be received by the public. After all, the Atlanta newspapers had already decreed that Payne's reputation was on the line, we reminded ourselves with our tongues firmly in our cheeks. While Billy Payne would be a part of the negotiating team, it was Pound's show. I noted in my records later an interesting fact about Billy. As the rest of us began to tense from the anticipation of the negotiations just a few hours hence, our CEO seemed to get more relaxed. It was an interesting contrast because when confronting small irritants that seemed to bother no one else, he could get very angry and extremely emotional. But when things were really serious, he was very calm and focused. I realized then that he was a good leader and would only get better.

The walk from the hotel to the offices where the negotiations were to take place was only a few short blocks. As we left the hotel, we were met by a gaggle of reporters and photographers from the three local network affiliates in Atlanta, who interviewed us as they walked backwards, never missing a beat. I wondered if that skill was taught in the journalism schools. It was quite impressive.

When we arrived, I was asked to brief the negotiating team on our media plans for the day, including how we would handle the announcement once a deal had been made with one of the networks. I was lectured by Barry Frank, a former network executive, who we had hired as a consultant. Frank told me that the room in which we were scheduled to hold the media conference was too small. Imagine my surprise at that news. He said there would be cameramen and producers and sound technicians, and they would be climbing all over themselves. He added to my irritation by telling me to trust him, that he knew what he was talking about. I have never wanted to strangle anyone as badly in my life as I did Frank, but then it would only delay our negotiations and that wouldn't be helpful to the bottom line. Besides, I am sure it made him feel better to let a hick from Atlanta know how things worked in the big city.

Next to hoping to get the money we needed to make our budget, our second wish was that ABC would win the bid. The local affiliate in Atlanta, WSB, was the old-line station in town and the most watched. Their management had pulled out all the stops when the announcement was made that the Games were coming to Atlanta and they had lobbied their ABC colleagues to be competitive. They were a part of the same family that owned the newspaper and there seemed to be no love lost between them—another reason for rooting for WSB. Alas, on the day of the negotiations, ABC changed chairmen.

When the bids were opened from the three networks, NBC had the top bid, $456 million. ABC was next at $440 million, and CBS, $415. The groups then presented individually. The negotiations went on all day. CBS was eliminated first. ABC raised its bid to $450 but would go no further. NBC hung tough. Pound tried to move the network up and was unsuccessful. The magic number was $456 million and NBC had won the rights to broadcast the Centennial Olympic Games in Atlanta. A key component of their bid was that the network had agreed to share revenue with us on all advertising sales over $615 million. That would eventually add $18 million to our bottom line.

In retrospect, I had thought of ABC as the "Olympic network," primarily because of Roone Arledge, who headed the network's sports department for a number of years, and Jim McKay, who we all remember from the Munich disaster in 1972. But, in fact, NBC had clearly taken the title. Dick Ebersol, the president of NBC Sports, had established the network as the sports heavyweight among the networks. I didn't know it at the time, but NBC was an excellent choice.

The media conference to announce the choice was chaotic. The decision was announced to those of us outside the negotiating room just after 7:00 PM and we were informed that the news conference would be in less than an hour. We had told the media that we would gather two hours after the decision. Bad choice. An NBC vice president, Ed Markey, and I wrote and reproduced a news release. We took the release and ran—not jogged—the four blocks to the hotel. Run. Like full speed. The conference had already started. I slid the materials to Pound and Payne and both used the remarks I had written as though they had been rehearsing all day.

The room was like a sauna. The place was packed. There was no air conditioning, and the hotel couldn't get it working. But the press conference went great and the coverage was good. This was a great boost to employee morale back in Atlanta. With the money from NBC and the European Broadcast Union, we had gotten enough financial commitment to secure our line of credit from NationsBank and approval to begin construction on Olympic Stadium.

Thanks to great deal makers like Joe Bankoff, of the law firm of King & Spalding and one of the original bid members, Horace Sibley, of the same firm, ACOG achieved record-breaking revenue from the sale of broadcast rights around the world—$900 million. Sixty percent—$568 million—went to the bottom line.

Most important to the relief of us all, Billy had secured his reputation. I'm sure the Atlanta newspapers had a party to celebrate that fact.

Our third major source of revenue was the sale of tickets and was the one in which the public would have the most influence. We had projected initially that tickets would be 15% of the total that we needed. It turned out to provide 25% of our revenues. There had always been optimism about ticket sales. Geography was a big factor. One half the population lives east of the Mississippi River and is within a two-hour plane trip to Atlanta. We believed there were be a great demand for tickets. In fact, we needed a great demand for tickets because we had over eleven million to sell—more than Los Angeles and Barcelona combined. Preliminary rounds of football (soccer) were going to be held in huge football (American) stadiums out of state as well as at the University of Georgia, in Athens. In addition, there would be plenty of tickets available at Atlanta-Fulton County Stadium for Olympic baseball. Even after lopping off several million dollars for sales outside the states, Olympic VIPs and sponsors, there was going to be an abundant supply of tickets. Our market surveys told us that some twenty-two million people had expressed a desire to attend, nearly half from the Southeast.

One of the many things that worked well at the Atlanta Committee was Billy Payne's focus on our ticket philosophy. Despite the financial pressures on the committee, Billy was interested in making the Games available to as many people as possible. Unlike professional sports teams, he was not out to gouge the public, even though the anticipated demand would make it tempting to do so. Ninety percent of the Atlanta tickets cost the same or less than tickets for the 1984 Games in Los

Angeles when adjusted for inflation and the cost of transporting ticket holders to their venue. That was remarkable given that consumer prices were up almost 60% in that same time period.

Granted the best ticket to the most sought after event, Opening Ceremonies, was $636, but 95% of the tickets would be $75 or less. This meant everybody who wanted to could experience an Olympic event. Of course, the *Atlanta Journal-Constitution* heralded our efforts with a headline saying, "Desirable Seats At Top Events Will Cost Plenty" and further intoned that, "The unavoidable truth is that your chances of getting tickets to, say the Opening Ceremony—particularly with nearly half the seats taken by VIPs, athletes, the media, and corporate sponsors—are only slightly better than your chances of winning the lottery." The paper was turning "negative spin" into an art form. Fortunately, most people ignored them. They were too happy at the idea of getting to see the Olympic Games in person.

Scott Anderson, who as managing director of games services was responsible for seeing that this enormous undertaking went smoothly, and was the most unflappable of us all. Maybe when no one was looking, he would close his door and scream but otherwise he appeared to be having a good time. Obviously, he knew what he was doing.

An important feature of our ticket program was to "couple" tickets to a variety of events. This would lessen the temptation of ticket buyers, including sponsors, to secure packages to only the high-demand events and leave the other sports with empty venues. We took our proposals to the IOC executive committee in Lausanne in June 1994. In his presentation to that group, Anderson was explaining the cost structure and the philosophy of our selling tickets to all events. "We will," he said, "require those who are buying tickets to 'major' sports to also purchase ticket to 'minor' sports as well."

Pal Schmitt, the IOC representative from Hungary and that country's ambassador to Spain, was one of the most pleasant of the Olympic hierarchy and seemed one of the least affected by his position. He listened politely to Anderson's explanation and then asked, "Could you define 'major' sport and 'minor' sport to me, please?"

I am sure Anderson had anticipated the question and was quick in response to Schmitt. "Of course," Scott obliged, " a major sport would be basketball and a minor sport would be fencing." It was then that things got very quiet in the room. It turns out that Schmitt was a former gold medallist in—you guessed it—fencing. As everyone held their breath, Schmitt grinned and said, "You may have your categories reversed. I would consider basketball a minor sport and fencing a major one."

With the package approved, we began an intensive campaign to educate the public on ordering the tickets which could be done in the spring of 1995. Information was contained in a forty-eight page, four-color brochure that had been tested prior to its production to ensure that it would be easy to fill out. The brochure also explained the accommodations policy. In addition, over thirty-six million brochures were available in 15,000 grocery stores carrying Coca-Cola products, and in Home Depot stores.

Response was instant and overwhelming. In the mail order phase from May to December 1995 of that year, we had sold over three million tickets. Where possible, we would fill a ticket request as submitted. Where events were oversubscribed (more requests than tickets available), we would attempt to get them in the same event but in a lower priced seat. Where that was not possible, the computer attempted to fill the customer's first or second alternative choice. Four out of five got at least one session they had requested. Most customers ordered an average of seventeen tickets; we averaged giving them nine. The second phase which lasted from February to the end of the Games, generated another 952,000 ticket sales.

This latter phase was responsible for one of the most popular stories about us. We were selling tickets within the United States only. If you were in another country, you had to order your tickets through that country. According to the story, a person called from New Mexico to inquire about ticket sales. The caller was told that we could not help; we could only sell tickets within the United States. "But I live in New Mexico," he exclaimed. "New Mexico or Old Mexico, you are still going to have to get your tickets there," was the reply. It was a great story and made the newspapers around the world. Just one problem: It seems the story may have been apocryphal. We could find no evidence of the conversation having taken place. In fact, a reporter from one of the national magazines said that same story had been told a number of times in the past. It seemed to stick to us because our friends in the local media liked to tweak us whenever possible and the national media believed the story indicative of our lack of sophistication. After all, they reasoned, we were from the Deep South.

Another unique feature of ACOG's ticket policy was that during the Games, one could buy available tickets at any venue for any other venue. In the past, you could only get tickets for that particular venue. Due to that fact, we sold as many as 35,000 tickets for next day events. We also employed mobile vans to sell tickets in other cities and sold over 40,000. You want to buy tickets? Scott Anderson would sell you tickets.

My biggest gaffe as a part of the management team revolved around the tickets and I have no one to blame but myself. As mentioned elsewhere, the state of Georgia had provided us extraordinary help and support that would, have they been a private corporation, qualified them as a major sponsor. We agreed that we would treat them like one. The Department of Industry and Trade, which is responsible for the state's economic development, wanted to use the Olympic marks in their advertising overseas. We agreed, with some minor conditions. So far, so good.

We then further sanctioned their sponsor-like status by allowing the administration and members of the General Assembly to do what our other sponsors did — turn in their order for tickets ahead of the sale to the general public. For good measure, we also added the mayor of Atlanta, the City Council and a number of state and local boards — about 400 all told. These tickets were to be drawn from a special cache set aside that had existed from the beginning for our sponsors and the sports federations and foreign Olympic committees. These tickets were not a part of the pool of tickets that were in the public allotment.

Like sponsors, they could get two tickets to opening or closing ceremonies, as well as two tickets to the high-demand events. The announcement that we were instituting this policy was made in May 1995, just as the general public phase was getting underway. The timing could not have been worse but in retrospect, there was no good time for it. People were outraged at the thought of politicians getting special treatment. The media also was aghast. A reporter from WSB-TV came huffing into my office, demanding an interview. "Who else," he barked, "gets preferential treatment from ACOG?"

"There's only one other group," I said, "and that's the media. They don't pay anything to get in." I can't recall today but I think that may have been cut out of the interview that ran that evening. Even without my *bon mot*, the story led their news that night and ran for eight minutes. If you don't think that is a long time, try holding your breath that long. Had I only eight minutes to live, I would want it to be when I was watching a story that bad for that long. I might feel like I was going to live forever.

When Melissa Turner called me from the newspaper, she was sure that somehow that decision had gotten by me. I was viewed as a control freak by the paper because I insisted that all media contacts come through my office and that no one, including Payne or Frazier, agree to an interview without my prior knowledge. Also, I had a strong hand on many of the policy decisions made at ACOG. Given that, the paper knew that someone had slipped up and done this extraordinarily dumb thing without consulting me. Imagine her shock to find out that I had been a party to the decision. All she could mutter was "I can't believe you approved that." All I could mutter in return was, "I can't either."

The firestorm was so predictable that had I been the CEO, I might have had me publicly flogged for not pointing out the downside. That is what I was paid to do. I had simply gotten too busy doing too many other things and dropped the ball. The flap did accomplish one thing, however. It gladdened my detractors in the media. As my Mama used to say, there is something good in everything.

As with our sponsorships and our broadcast rights sales, ticket sales were a great success, financially and otherwise. Through the efforts of Anderson and his people, ticket sales exceeded $462 million. ACOG had sold over eight million tickets. My favorite statistic is that we sold more tickets to women's events alone than Barcelona sold tickets for their entire Games. We even sold more baseball tickets than Lillehammer had sold tickets for the Winter Games of 1996. While there were a few glitches, and a lot of happy people who will long remember with pleasure attending the 1996 Centennial Olympic Games.

Looking back now, it is difficult to recall just how precarious that Financial Tightrope Walking competition was. I suspect that Billy Payne, A. D. Frazier, Pat Glisson, and others will never forget. They were the ones who were operating on the tightwire. As Frazier will now admit, "There were days I wasn't sure where the money was coming from."

I'm glad he waited until after the Games to tell me that. As I speak around the country about how we—not me, but Payne, Frazier, McCahan, Anderson, Bankoff, Moss, et al.—raised $1.7 billion privately, built the things we did, did the things we did, and didn't have to be bailed out by government, people are shocked. Now that I think about it, I am too.

# 5

## BUILDING SUSPICIONS

I am sure there have been times in your life when you have said something you later regret having said. I have done that more times than I wish to remember.

However, there is one particular moment that stands above the rest. On a beautiful Monday morning in March 1995, I was standing in the front yard of a home in Myrtle Beach, South Carolina, looking at the ocean and said to no one in particular, "I feel great."

No one associated with the planning of Olympic Games should ever make such a statement, and I, particularly, should have known better but I couldn't help it. I did feel great.

My wife Jane and I had spent the weekend with our neighbors and close friends Tom and Jane Hoover at their vacation home in Myrtle Beach. The weekend had consisted of watching a lot of basketball on television, walking on the beach, some outlet shopping (but not too much), eating seafood, visiting an old friend, country star Larry Gatlin, who (along with his brothers) has a theater there, and, most of all, sleeping. I had arrived on Friday in my usual frazzled state but by Monday morning, I was a new man.

Having uttered those fateful words, I happily climbed in the backseat of the Hoovers' automobile and prepared to return to the grind in Atlanta, some six hours away.

Fifteen minutes into the trip my pager buzzed. It was Donna Johnsson, my deputy. I knew it had to be urgent; otherwise, Donna would not bother me. An executive with Southern Company, she was on loan to the committee but had proven to be such an excellent manager that we asked her to come on board fulltime. The longer she was there, the more responsibility she assumed in the public relations department, freeing me up to work on the government relations side. There wasn't much in our department that Ms. Johnsson couldn't handle with her own good judgment. If she was paging me, it had to be serious.

I called her back on my cell phone to learn that one of the light stanchions in our Olympic Stadium under construction had collapsed and a workman had been killed and two others injured. I still remember as I got the details from Donna, secretly cursing myself for having ever said how great I felt. With one phone call, the relaxing weekend was now history. There was pandemonium in Atlanta and I was six hours away.

Tom and Jane Hoover have been great friends for two decades. We have shared some wonderful times together and have supported each other through some tough times. But there was nothing in our friendship that had prepared them for the trip back to Atlanta. I was on my cellular phone getting updates and assessing the impact of the accident. I was also trying to locate Billy Payne, who was in California, to see how much he knew and to discuss the next steps. It was more than my cell phone could manage and it soon gave up the ghost.

Fortunately, I spied Tom's phone in the front seat. As president of a steel supply company in Atlanta, he was often on the road and needed a phone to check into his office. There was no time for decorum. While he drove as if a participant in the Daytona 500, I commandeered his phone, pulled the cord into the backseat and picked up where I had left off. After dodging the telephone cord a number of times as I careened around in the back seat, Jane Hoover volunteered to let me sit up front for the rest of the trip. No friendship is worth strangulation by a telephone cord.

To this day, I don't know who was more relieved to be back in Atlanta; me, because of my need to be involved immediately in the next steps we would need to take, or the Hoovers, who were silently thanking their lucky stars to be rid of the crisis — and me.

As is the case in most construction fatalities, the immediate cause was not known and we were careful not to speculate until the facts were in. In the meantime, the accident was worldwide news. In Atlanta, it was front-page news and the local stations gave the story from eight to twelve minutes. By contrast, when a worker tragically fell to his death in 1980 during the construction of Southern Bell's forty-five story headquarters building in Atlanta, it got one paragraph in the local paper and barely a mention on television.

After months of investigation, it was determined that a design flaw had caused the light tower to collapse. In layman's language, the bank of lights on the tower was originally calculated to weigh less than it actually did, and the structure was designed for the lighter weight. The towers were redesigned.

The collapse of the light stanchion was a clear setback to a project that had been dogged with controversy from the start. More than any other event in the planning process, the construction of the Olympic Stadium tore away the façade of Atlanta as defined by its chamber of commerce hype and exposed the city for what it is: a town with an enormous racial divide and governed by politicians who are captives to the special interests spawned by racial politics.

The business community seems powerless to change the situation and the local media, in my opinion, has neither the ability nor the desire to be the catalyst to alter the status quo. The contentiousness that accompanied the approval of the stadium deal was the singular moment when we became conscious of the fact that we weren't as big a city—in every respect—as we thought we were. There would be no more ticker-tape parades in Atlanta. Reality had set in. As always, it was Billy Payne who said it best, "I didn't realize how hard it would be to give away a $209 million stadium."

Nothing caused more public anxiety in the early days of the planning process than our construction progress—or lack of it. People wondered where all the structures were. Why wasn't anything coming out of the ground? Can you be finished on time? Even members of the International Olympic Committee were not above expressing their concerns. One of Billy Payne's best lines to those who did was, "Don't worry. We build stuff faster than you do." He was right. We did.

We also developed a mantra: "On Time, On Target, On Schedule." It was something I had learned over the years. Simple messages, said often and consistently. We put that line in everything we did. Once as Billy Payne was winding down a press conference, Bert Roughton of the *Atlanta Journal Constitution* asked, "Billy, you haven't told us today. Are you on time, on target, on schedule?" It got a good laugh from everybody, including Billy.

Our plans called for the construction of some $500 million in new facilities and the adaptation of a number of existing venues. Nearly half that amount would be budgeted for the Olympic Stadium, location of the opening and closing ceremonies, track and field, and the start and finish of the marathon.

A new tennis center, archery center, and cycling velodrome were scheduled for Stone Mountain Park, some fifteen miles east of the city. Originally, Stone Mountain was to be the location for Olympic rowing as well until someone discovered that the lake's small size would require some competitors to row on land. Rowing was moved to Gainesville, forty miles to the northeast. The archery and velodrome sites were removed after the Games because no one wanted them, leaving a $15 million state-of-the-art tennis facility with an 8,000-seat center court and fifteen practice courts.

Another example of facilities that would be beneficial after the Games was the aquatic center. Swimming is not a major collegiate sport but it is one of the marquee events of the Olympic Games. To accommodate both situations, ACOG built a $25 million facility on the campus of Georgia Tech. It would accommodate for the first time all Olympic aquatic sports—diving, swimming, synchronized swimming and water polo. More importantly, it would seat 16,000 during the Games and then covert to a 3000-seat stadium to be given to Georgia Tech for their use.

In addition, it produced the dumbest question I ever heard at a media briefing. In thirty-five years, I thought I had heard them all. To ensure that our Olympic venues would be as ready as possible for the Centennial Games, we had held a number of "test events" the year before. "Test events" was a misnomer because in some cases, the competitions were for world championships and to qualify for the upcoming Games. This included the Pan Pacific Swimming Championships at the Aquatics Center. A number of records had been broken in the pool by world-class athletes. It had been thrilling to watch and to know this was the level of competition we could anticipate at the Olympic Games.

The week after the event, Billy Payne held a briefing to update the media on the success of the test events, including the competitions at Georgia Tech. Hearing about the records that had been broken at the Aquatic Center, one reporter raised his hand and asked earnestly, "Billy, do you have any concerns that the water at Georgia Tech may be too fast?" The usually quick-thinking Payne was too dumbfounded to answer.

New facilities were also constructed in the fast-growing city of Conyers, thirty miles east of Atlanta to host all the equestrian competitions: dressage, show jumping and the three-day event. ACOG put in some $20 million and Conyers another $15 million. Located on 1139 acres and owned by the city of Conyers, it is now known as the Georgia International Equestrian Center, one of the premiere facilities of its type in the country.

Atlanta is the home of the Atlanta University Center, composed of a group of predominantly black colleges, including Morehouse (alma mater of Dr. Martin Luther King, Jr.), Morris Brown, Clark Atlanta, Spelman, and the Interdenominational Theological Center, all located side by side. Both Clark Atlanta and Morris Brown got new football stadiums as a result of Olympic facilities used for field hockey. Morehouse received a new gymnasium that had been used for preliminary rounds of men and women's basketball competitions. Spelman wasn't ignored. The woman's college acquired a major exhibit, courtesy of the Cultural Olympiad.

The Wolf Creek Shooting Complex, located south of Atlanta, was the venue for the fifteen medal events in Olympic Shooting. That facility went to Fulton County, which in my opinion should have been ashamed to accept it, given their lack of support throughout the planning process. Even today, they still owe $600,000.

To accommodate the athletes from 197 countries, the state of Georgia constructed new facilities on the campus of Georgia Tech, not far from the Aquatic Center and within two miles of sixteen competition venues. There were a number of satellite villages in the cities outside Atlanta that were hosting competitions. Our agreement with the state was that we would rent back the facilities for the time of the Games and then they would be converted to dormitories for students at Tech and Georgia State University, an urban institution located just south of Georgia Tech.

Finally, a yachting venue was constructed at Wassaw Sound on the Georgia coast near Savannah. It was struck twice by lightning during construction, and hit by Hurricane Bertha eight days before competition was to start. I can only assume that God isn't a yachting fan.

Beyond the new construction, ACOG adapted existing structures and facilities for the additional venues that were required. These included the

Georgia Dome, home of the Atlanta Falcons, the Omni, home at the time for the Atlanta Hawks, coliseums at Georgia Tech, Georgia State, and the University of Georgia, the World Congress Center, a massive state facility in downtown Atlanta, Atlanta-Fulton County Stadium and Sanford Stadium at the University of Georgia. The latter venue was of particular concern to Billy Payne and to me.

Football reigns supreme on Saturday afternoons in the fall. Nowhere is that more true than in Athens, Georgia, home of the Georgia Bulldogs. I am admittedly prejudiced, but I think Sanford Stadium is one of the most beautiful stadiums in the country. Its most prominent feature is a hedge that encircles the field and leads to the boast that the Dawgs will whip anybody they get "between the hedges."

At the time Billy announced that the finals of men's and women's Olympic soccer would be held at Sanford Stadium, I was president of the UGA national alumni association. In order to convert the field for soccer, the playing area would have to be larger than an American football field, meaning that (gasp!) thehedges would have to be removed and since the Bulldogs would start up their season within a month of the end of the Centennial Games, they would have to be replaced or there would be hell to pay with the alumni.

The task of telling the UGA faithful fell to Georgia Athletic Director Vince Dooley. At a news conference in Athens, Coach Dooley, a cautious man by nature, assured the loyalists that the old hedge was already in the process of dying and would have needed to be removed anyway, soccer or no soccer, and would be replaced by new plants every bit as good, maybe even better than the old ones. His sincerity was impressive as again and again he noted the dire condition of the old hedges, in case any alumni had missed his point the first time.

As he intoned further the sad state of the sickly hedges, his effervescent wife, Barbara, who enjoys tweaking her husband's somber public persona, began to sing softly in the back of the room (but loud enough for Vince to hear) to the tune of Ol' Man River, "Those Poor Old Hedges; Those Poor Old Hedges. They All Are Dying. They All Are Dying." There was hardly a dry eye in the room, not from sadness but because we were all laughing so hard. The only one who failed to appreciate the humor was Coach Dooley.

Not all of the venues were built or modified by us. Atlanta Beach, located south of Atlanta was developed by Clayton County for beach volleyball. The city of Columbus, 100 miles southwest of Atlanta, offered Golden Park for women's fast pitch softball, and the U.S. Forest Service constructed the first natural whitewater slalom course in Olympic history on the Ocoee River near Cleveland, Tennessee.

Managing the enormous complexity of these high-profile projects fell on the shoulders of Bill Moss, managing director of construction. As stated before, everybody at the senior management level and down throughout the organization at the Atlanta Committee was a top professional in their field. Looking back at the key players today, it is my opinion that each of us could have been replaced with someone just as good or better, with one exception — Bill Moss.

Like most construction people I have met over the years, Bill was a no-nonsense individual who brooked no interference from anyone, including his bosses. His philosophy seemed to be, "If you want to build it, then do it, but if you want me to build it, then get out of my business." He came to the committee at the invitation of Bob Holder, co-chairman of the Board, who had worked with him on a project at Universal Studios in Orlando, Florida. While Moss had no love for the press, he was one of the best to sit down with reporters when we requested it and brief them on construction issues. He had high credibility with the media because of his straight-forward style. He was also very good to work with internally because as we appreciated what he did and knew not to tell him how to do it, so he seemed to understand our responsibilities and wasn't interested in becoming a public relations "expert."

Moss's first critical assignment was to supervise the construction of the Olympic Stadium. It would be the most visible and the most costly of all the projects. Before he could build the stadium, however, the stadium design and budget had to first be approved. Getting that done quickly brought to the surface the always-simmering racial tensions in town. Negotiations were protracted, and petty politics almost cost Atlanta its current stadium. At one point there were serious thoughts of building a temporary stadium outside the city for the Atlanta Games and tearing the whole thing down afterwards. Nothing in the agreement forced us to build within the city limits.

Leading the negotiations for ACOG was A. D. Frazier, ACOG's chief operating officer and his staff. Having arrived at ACOG at the most contentious point of the debate, I made what I hoped would be the first of many suggestions to Payne about the external environment. I wanted him to lower his profile during the negotiations. At that point, three-and-one-half years prior to the Games, Billy was still a lightning rod to many people in town. He had seen the initial euphoria dissipate into quarrels over a myriad of issues, and he was testy over the fact that many people who had supported the bid were now trying to split the economic pie to their advantage.

Because of my corporate environment experience, I have some very definite beliefs on what the CEO's role should be. The CEO should be on the front lines when there is very bad news or very good news. That is why you saw Billy Payne when the light tower collapsed and when the bomb exploded in Centennial Park, as well as when we announced the addition of a major sponsor. But he didn't need to be in the middle of the complex and highly politicized stadium negotiations. There were enough problems in getting the stadium deal approved without adding his frustrations to the equation. Billy's role as a CEO was changing rapidly from someone who could be involved in the most minute details of a small group to an executive in charge of one of the most complex organizations in the world. This was not your average American corporation.

The Atlanta Braves had been making noises that, unless they got a new stadium, they would be moving out of downtown and to the suburbs where developers would be happy to accommodate them. A new stadium would keep them in the heart of the city. In the bid for the Olympic Games, the bid committee promised to build a stadium that would be converted to a baseball stadium after the Games.

After examining several sites, the committee chose the parking lot south of and adjacent to Atlanta-Fulton County stadium. Negotiations for the new stadium took over a year and involved the city of Atlanta, Fulton County, the Braves, the Atlanta-Fulton County Recreation Authority who owned the property, as well as the politically-powerful neighborhood groups around the stadium. It was adversarial from the start. There were a number of issues to be ironed out from what kind of facility was to be built to who was going to pay for what, to guaranteeing minority employment to revenue sharing to paying off the bonds on the old stadium and tearing it down. Ultimately the deal went through but the excitement and the magic were gone by the time it was finalized. Petty politics reigned and nowhere more than at the Atlanta-Fulton County Recreation Authority.

The Atlanta-Fulton County Recreation Authority, composed of elected officials and local citizens, managed the current stadium and made a big issue of taxpayer liability for the upkeep of the new stadium once the Games were over. In listening to the hyperbole emanating from this group, you would have thought the facility would be a rusted hulk by August 5, the day after closing ceremonies. It was clearly an attempt to milk a perceived cash cow for all it was worth and a chance to take a cheap shot at the Committee for their "no taxpayer funds for the Games."

Board members, specifically Mary Rose Taylor, a former local newscaster, and Tom Lowe, long-time member of the Fulton County Commission, were trying to frighten the public with dire predictions of taxpayer catastrophe. Lowe opined, "I see us leaving a legacy awash with debt, red ink, and disaster that will last until my grandchildren have grandchildren." What was his problem? He wanted the Braves to put more money into maintenance after they assumed operating responsibility. From somewhere, he had concocted a $500 million cost of maintenance and repair for the stadium over the next 40 years. I found his numbers dubious, as did most people. I thought his arguments spurious then and I find them spurious today.

Lowe boasted to the Atlanta newspapers that he believed he had enough votes on the Commission to kill the deal, even though all the other signatories had signed off on it. He didn't, of course. He ended up voting for it himself.

While its members were running around like Chicken Little to see if the sky was falling because of this $209 million state-of-the-art stadium that had landed in their lap, in early 1995 the executive director of the authority, Davetta Johnson, was appealing to Frazier to "advance" the group $1.5 million to buy a piece of property adjacent to the stadium that would be used for parking during the Games and for housing afterwards. (I would point out that it is still a parking lot five years later.) The Recreation Authority had $1.5 million of its own money, but was restricted from using the money for anything other than paying down the bonds on Atlanta-Fulton County Stadium. If Frazier would grant their request, the authority would deduct that same amount from what we would be required to pay on the bonds, since ACOG was assuming responsibility for retiring the debt on the old stadium. After much conversation, Frazier agreed in good faith to the deal, only to be told a couple of months later that the board would not approve her arrangement. The committee, therefore, was out $1.5 million, and the Authority had their parking lot and $1.5 million in reserve which would never see the light of day since ACOG would be paying off the bonds on the old stadium for them.

The issue of race wasn't long in making its mark on the stadium negotiations. At the time of the stadium negotiations, most of the senior management was white and lived in the more affluent north side of Atlanta. This led to charges that we were insensitive to the needs of the inner city poor and to minorities in general. It all came to a head when Martin Luther King, III, the eldest son and namesake of the famed civil rights leader, and a member of the Fulton County commission condemned our stadium agreement and blistered us publicly. He was particularly incensed at what he thought was a lack of interest on our part in giving the Atlanta University Center colleges a bigger role in the Games. Before he was through, the Braves had capped taxpayer liability for capital improvement and renovations to the stadium at $50 million, and had agreed to share parking revenues with the neighborhoods. For our part, we acceded to his demand that a top black administrator report directly to Billy Payne. Happily for all of us, that turned out to be Shirley Franklin, an outstanding individual. The AUC ended up with $51 million and we pledged to spend $150,000 on a job-training program for residents of the neighborhoods around the stadium.

With that, young Mr. King went back to a remarkably undistinguished career as a commission member and was promptly defeated when he ran for commission chairman. But he had made a lasting mark on the Atlanta Commitee.

So, the stadium was finally approved but the resentment and mistrust on both sides—ACOG and the local governments—continued through the rest of the planning period and the Games themselves. They thought us arrogant; we thought them incompetent.

As time for construction approached in July 1993, we faced the predictable union threats regarding how the stadium was going to get built. Our general contractor, Beers Construction, had a pretty good relationship with the local trades, but the national people were interested in using the Olympics as a kind of staging area to rejuvenate the union movement. This was nothing new. Every special-interest group with an axe to grind saw us as the world's largest microphone, and attempted to use us accordingly. This trend would only escalate during the years and months leading up to the Centennial Games.

We were able to work out a compromise with the trade unions after a couple of false starts, and were ready to break ground on July 10 with much fanfare. In the excitement of the moment, we placed an ad announcing the groundbreaking and inviting the public to the ceremonies. The ad was illustrated with a picture of someone's leg forcing a shovel in the ground. Richard Monteilh, the staff director of MAOGA, who was supposed to be watching our finances suddenly added the duties of advertising expert. He called me in a dither because while you could only see the leg from the knee down, it was, according to Richard, "white and hairy." He said blacks would get upset at seeing a white leg and women would be upset at seeing hair. So, rather than ask him where he had gotten his market research, I put sweat pants on the leg and left it to the public to figure out what kind of leg it was. I was halfway expecting a call to see if the pants had been made in some sweatshop in Southeast Asia.

Despite the political correctness, the groundbreaking was a major event. We had a group of protestors, of course, but there were so few and they were so far away and it was so hot that the media ignored them, much to their chagrin. Joe Boone, a local activist and long in the tooth, rushed on stage and seized the microphone. We promptly cut off the sound system and let him speak. No one paid any attention to him. Somebody forgot to get word to the unions that an agreement had been reached. Two planes flew overhead with banners reading, "No Contract. No Peace." and "No Contract. No Olympics." while union workers were celebrating the last minute agreement.

Mainly, the attendees were plain, ordinary folk, black and white, young and old, rich and poor, drawn together by the fact that a stadium was finally coming out of the ground. That meant the Olympic Games were coming. For a brief moment, we all forgot the unpleasantness that we incurred to get us there.

There would be other controversies. The new dormitories being built by the state would sink up to nine inches and stop and—dire predictions to the contrary—were terrific additions to the athlete's village. They now house Georgia State students.

There would be wind damage to the Aquatic Center and a crack developed at the Olympic Stadium. None of these incidents were major and all of the facilities have enjoyed four years of use by the taxpayers of Georgia.

The construction program was a great legacy to a city and county that seemed less than grateful to have them. I agree with my friend Billy Payne. Not only is it hard to give away $209 million, but it is even more odious when you think who you are giving it to.

# 6

## GOVERNMENT WORKS

One of the more familiar mantras of the 1996 Games was "no government funding." While Billy Payne and his small band of volunteers had stunned the world by getting the Centennial Olympics for Atlanta, he would never have had the opportunity if there had been any thought of the city or the State of Georgia obligating taxpayers to build and operate the facilities necessary to put on the Games. That was not even remotely possible.

Peter Ueberroth, the genius behind the incredibly successful 1984 Los Angeles Olympics, had all but precluded government funds being used to stage the Games in the United States when he instituted a hugely-successful program to sell sponsorship categories to a limited number of major corporations. The price tag in 1984 was $4 million. By the time, Atlanta's turn rolled around twelve years later, the asking price for Olympic sponsorships was ten times that. But where the cost of putting on LA's Games was estimated to be around $500 million, Atlanta was projecting its costs at $1.6 billion. But those dollars would cover what we called, "inside the fence," meaning putting on the Games themselves. It did not include those things that were the obvious responsibility of the various levels of government—local, state, and federal—security, traffic control, immigration, weather forecasting, tourism, transportation, and the like. Saying that we would put on the Games without government support was incorrect. We were going to need between $30 million and $50 million from the government "outside the fence." The trick was to decide how much was "normal levels" and how much we should be expected to compensate the various governments for their extraordinary expenses.

Beyond the price tag was the complication of dealing with a host of government bodies in all the areas where we were holding competitions or events, as well as the various agencies within those bodies and their relationships with each other.

In early 1994, I was assigned the additional duty of coordinating the state and federal government relationships, while my colleague, Shirley Franklin, would work the city of Atlanta and the local, city, and county governments in the metropolitan Atlanta area. If you aren't careful, one governmental group will play you off against another one. Coordination inside ACOG was essential both between Shirley and me and between the two of us and the other departments.

While we had a number of people in the organization with political experience at all levels of government, it was gratifying that no one got in the way of the government relations function. Most understood what a hard task I had and went out of their way to be helpful. Maybe everybody was too busy with their own responsibilities or maybe we just attracted the kind of people who were so confident in their abilities, and had enough confidence in mine, that there was no need to meddle. Given the high stress factor and the almost impossible deadlines, we did not need a lot of people messing in our business, and happily it did not happen.

My first duty was to get the government relations responsibility away from the Metropolitan Atlanta Olympic Games Authority and its executive director, Richard Monteihl, who had assumed that responsibility for himself. MAOGA was chartered to approve and sign the multi-year commitments needed to construct the Olympic facilities. They had also assumed an oversight role to monitor our financial progress and to ensure that taxpayer dollars were not used inside the fence. I did not see anything in their mandate that gave Monteihl political oversight, too.

I had inherited good people. Lindsay Thomas had been a five-term member of Congress from Georgia's First District, and tired of the petty politics and constant fund-raising required to maintain that seat, had joined ACOG a year or so earlier. Working with him was Cindy Gillespie, who had spent much of her young career on the lobbying side of politics, and had a terrific grasp of details. I immediately split their duties and assigned Thomas to state politics and Gillespie to Washington. It played to their strengths. Thomas is very engaging, well liked and was perfectly suited to the personal lobbying in the State House. In addition, it was flattering to members of the state legislature to have a former member of Congress calling on them.

Gillespie, on the other hand, was a workaholic who could keep up with the myriad details of untold federal agencies and Congressional committees which had claimed some responsibility for some facet of our Games.

Our most critical need was security. We had 15,000 athletes and officials coming from 197 countries along with 15,000 media representatives, 25,000 members of the "Olympic family," and assorted VIPs. We were also forecasting some two million visitors. In short, we would have a lot of people—many foreign nationals—in a concentrated area for a relatively short period of time.

We felt vulnerable because neither the city nor the state had enough manpower to meet our needs, even by borrowing law enforcement personnel from other cities. They could offer hundreds. We needed thousands. I am told that Los Angeles County has more officers off-duty on any day than there were active officers in the State of Georgia. In addition, there was not enough local dollars available to cover the personnel costs and we would have to look to the federal government to try and cover the shortfall which we estimated to be some $8 million.

Security planning was being coordinated by the Olympic Security Support Group (OSSG), comprised of representatives of all law enforcement agencies and entities with security responsibility. It seemed a cast of thousands. Its members included the Department of Defense, the FBI, the Secret Service, the INS, the Georgia State Patrol, the Georgia Bureau of Investigation, the Atlanta Police Department, the Fulton County Sheriff's Office, and more than thirty other law enforcement agencies. Clearly, the lead agency was the Department of Defense. We wanted DOD personnel, particularly the military, to help in areas like perimeter security, bag searches, traffic control, medical evacuation if needed, and a host of other duties. We would also need materials ranging from radios to fencing.

On another front, we spent a number of months dealing with the Department of Justice on the Americans With Disabilities Act (ADA). I cannot recall a law that has better intentions and is more convoluted than ADA. The Justice Department was caught in the middle between hard-line advocates who wanted to use the Olympic Games as a show piece for their cause and a potential political fallout that would come from suing us over some issues as inane as having handicap access in the dugouts of our main stadium once it was converted to a baseball stadium after the Games. That the highly volatile issue got worked out to the satisfaction of all the parties, including us, was a credit to the Civil Rights Division of the Department of Justice. To say I was surprised at their positive attitude, after all I had heard about them, is an understatement.

There were other issues to be dealt with as well. The federal Department of Transportation was scouring the country for buses to transport athletes, spectators and the media. One of the ongoing concerns of the public was whether or not Atlanta would be gridlocked during the three weeks of the Games. I understood their concern but wondered why they accepted the ongoing gridlock every other day of their lives. Certainly, nobody at City Hall seemed interested in the gridlock caused by the infamous Freaknik celebration, a black college spring break revelry that totally closed down the city one weekend in April each year.

In August 1994, we rolled out our transportation plan. We were hoping to get some 2000 new, air-conditioned buses from the Department of Transportation. We planned to paint them and return them to the cities from which they came with a plaque saying that the bus had participated in the 1996 Centennial Olympic Games in Atlanta.

We needed special consideration from the Department of Justice and the State Department to get the athletes, officials, and journalists from 197 countries into the United States on an expedited basis, and to screen the candidates in as non-intrusive manner as possible. This would include dealing with nations with whom we do not have diplomatic relations, including Cuba, Iraq, Iran, and Afghanistan. There was a strong distrust of U.S. Government among IOC members and concerns about whether we would politicize entry into the country. Frankly, I was concerned, too. Except for one instance, the federal government was extremely helpful. Sometimes the simple things will trip you up. One of the big expectations of the IOC was the spouses' lunch with the First Lady at the White House just prior to the Games. This was three years after we had been through complex negotiations on transportation issues, funding issues, security issues, coordination issues. We thought we were to the easy part. We were wrong.

The National Security Council refused to allow members from the eight nations with whom we have no diplomatic relations to attend the reception—Olympics or not. The real focus was Libya and Yugoslavia. Libya was a particularly emotional issue with the NSC because of their suspected role in the downing of PanAm flight 103 more than seven years earlier. We dodged a major international incident when the spouses from those two countries declined their invitation.

There were to be foreign nationals employed by NBC, our U.S. rights holder, and they require special approval by the Department of Labor. Because weather is always tenuous in Atlanta, the National Weather Service was needed to provide us the most sophisticated forecasting possible to prevent having a stadium full of people and tornados at the same time.

The list seemed endless.

In truth, we were not asking for hard dollars as much as we were seeking human resources, equipment, and support but when our wish list was tallied up it came to some $200 million dollars of state and federal support. The local, state, and federal governments combined spent closer to $800 million in preparation for the Atlanta Games but beyond direct support for our needs, most of the money went to improvements that would have been made anyway, such as getting our interstate system ready—it was the first time in forty years that some part of our massive interstate system around Atlanta did not have some part under construction or repair—electronic road signage, a new Martin Luther King, Jr. visitors center, and massive airport improvements. The Games conveniently moved up all of the timetables.

Any support from the state and federal governments would be infinitely more than we would get from the City of Atlanta. In the first place, the city did not have much to offer, and their focus seemed to be less on helping us than on trying to get as much as possible from us. Their demands bordered on the ridiculous and they were the weakest link of the governmental chain. They were also the most uncooperative.

Succeeding in our quest of government support would be difficult, but we had a lot of things in our favor. First, the Clinton Administration seemed genuinely interested in helping. It was not lost on me that 1996 was also an election year and a happy electorate would be to the president's advantage. However, I am convinced their involvement could have been "top-down" and bullying had they chosen to do so, but it was not.

For that, I credit Thomas F. (Mack) McLarty. Mack was officially counselor to the president and in the early days of the administration had been chief of staff. More importantly, he was from Hope, Arkansas, and had gone from grammar school through high school with Bill Clinton and remained one of the president's closest friends. He is a man of impeccable integrity and a true Southern gentleman. (Unlike the plethora of name-droppers that all presidential administrations seem to spawn, I do not think I heard Mack refer to his special friendship with the president more than twice in the three years I worked with him. He did not have to. Everybody knew.) I shudder to think of what we would have done without Mack McLarty as the Clinton Administration's point man.

The president is a huge sports fan and the Atlanta Games were of great personal interest to him. He also genuinely liked Billy Payne and took great delight in reminding our CEO of his last game as a Georgia Bulldog: Arkansas defeated them in the 1969 Sugar Bowl, 16-2.

Vice President Gore was appointed to chair an interagency task force of major federal departments with any role to play in the Games, and to my surprise, was an active player. I assumed he would show up for the photo ops and then disappear, but that was not the case. His attention to detail was impressive. I have been around politics long enough to know when someone has been briefed coming in the door and when they actually know their subject. Gore fits in the latter category. We learned early on to do our homework before we met with the vice president because he knew a lot about our business.

I never ceased to be amazed watching the transformation Gore went through as the number of people in his presence grew. In a group of three or four, he was personable, very much at ease and could be extremely witty. (Yes, witty.) But if the group got larger than that, the stiff manner that we have all come to associate with Gore would transform him and he would turn wooden. It never failed in all the times I was around him.

While the administration played a critical role in the federal government's cooperation, we also needed the support of the Congress. Again, we were in luck. The Speaker of the House, Newt Gingrich, was a Georgian, and while he and the Clinton Administration disagreed about almost everything, in this case they were in complete accord. Both wanted good games in Atlanta, if for different reasons. For Gingrich, who was not as popular statewide as one might assume a sitting Speaker of the House would be, it was a chance to validate his credentials as a Georgian, not a national political figure.

We tested the Speaker's patience by moving a volleyball venue out of his district because of protests from gay rights advocates over a "family values" resolution passed by the Cobb County Commission and by not running the Olympic torch through the county for the same reason. He was furious at us for what he considered to be our caving in to a small and vocal minority. Later, to his credit, he became a major player in guiding our requests through the House.

Our interests also were well represented in the Senate. Since much of our focus was on security, we were fortunate that the ranking minority member of the Armed Service committee was Georgia's senior senator, Sam Nunn. Being a member of the minority party in no way diminished his considerable influence. Without question, Nunn was one of the most respected members of that body on both sides of the aisle.

Nunn was important not only in our legislative efforts, but he knew the military better than most people in the Pentagon. He would tell us quickly if there was anything in our requests that was not feasible. He was, and remains, a great admirer of Billy Payne and wanted to see Georgia do well in the world's spotlight. Yet he was very practical, even cautious, and continued to seek assurances from us that we were being politically astute in our dealings in Washington. We were very sensitive of his reputation, and worked hard not to take advantage of his friendship and help. As with Mack McLarty in the White House, I am not sure what we would have done without Sam Nunn in the Senate.

Less known, but just as important to our efforts, was the state's junior senator, Paul Coverdell. In case you are not familiar with his name, it is for good reason. He works behind the scenes, and while he has a relatively low profile nationally, he has very quietly accumulated an impressive amount of clout with his fellow Republicans in the Senate. It was Coverdell who had the unpleasant job of dealing with John McCain, his Republican colleague from Arizona.

McCain's dislike for us was genuine (and mutual) and had as its genesis the World Cup, which had been held in Los Angeles in 1994. For that event, Congress had authorized $50 million, most of it for security support. The World Cup was a success in every respect, including finances. The chairman of the organizing committee authorized huge bonuses, including $7 million for himself. McCain was enraged at the audacity of the organizers. In his mind, much of the financial success of those games was the result of money the federal government had contributed. He felt strongly the money should have been paid back to the government, not given as bonuses to the World Cup organizers. When that was unsuccessful, he proceeded to take out his frustrations on the Atlanta Committee. We didn't intend to pay bonuses. We had stated that a number of times. At this point, making a profit wasn't looking like a big issue. We were just hoping to break even. We were trying to protect several million highly vulnerable people at a very high profile time. That seemed not to matter to him.

It also didn't seem to matter that the committee did not become involved in the law enforcement side of the planning. That was between law enforcement agencies. Where we did request non-security materials, we would reimburse. That was the law.

McCain began a campaign of disinformation that his friends in the national media happily complied with. He claimed that we were planning to use military personnel for cooking and "providing laundry services to Olympic athletes." That was not true and to the best of my knowledge, McCain knew it was not true. Twice, ABC sent a reporter from Washington to report on our purported misuse of the military. The first time, we convinced him that his information was just plain wrong. Satisfied, he went back to Washington, only to be sent back to do a story anyway, and managed to include a nice sound bite from Senator McCain.

While changing planes in Chicago, I was paged and told that William Safire, the Washington columnist for the *New York Times* was looking for me. Wow! It doesn't get much better than that, I thought. Talking to a guy whose writing I had admired for so long. When I reached him by phone in the concourse at O'Hare, he asked me the predictable questions about our using the military for washing and cooking for the athletes. Guess who he had been talking to?

After dutifully explaining the facts and hoping I had made some headway, I saw his column a few days later in which he launched an attack on the Clinton Administration for using the Atlanta Games for political advantage and raising questions about our use of federal resources. While he quoted me in the column, I had the feeling most of it had been written before he ever talked to me. My disappointment was tempered when Lyn May, my media relations person, reminded me that Safire, after all, had been a speechwriter for Richard Nixon.

In August 1994, McCain introduced an amendment to a Department of Defense appropriations bill to require us to repay the federal government for any security costs incurred in putting on the Olympic Games in Atlanta. He lost 77-21.

In the meantime, the Republicans swept the House and Senate. Sam Nunn was no longer chairman of the Armed Services Committee. John McCain was now in the driver's seat.

In March 1995, McCain again introduced an amendment disallowing funding of "non-security" activities, such as the Olympics. This time it was obvious he didn't have the votes, so he dropped it. But he wasn't through.

In June 1995 McCain removed our funding and it was restored in a committee markup. He tried again in August 1995 and was beaten more soundly than the first time, 80-20. Gingrich had told us even if McCain got something out of the Senate for us not to worry; any DOD appropriations would have to go to a joint Senate-House conference committee and the Speaker said he would appoint only House members to that committee that would support us. After the way the Speaker had reacted to our Cobb County decisions, I was surprised and pleased.

In February 1996, McCain faxed a letter to Billy dusting off the old charge that we would use military for cooking and washing athletes' clothes. It wasn't a nice letter. He then went to the Senate floor to denounce us in the most vitriolic terms.

Sam Nunn was instrumental in getting the decision-making for security out of the hands of a mid-level bureaucrat in the Department of Defense and into the Department of the Army, where we all felt the matter belonged. Getting the responsibility in the Army was a major step forward. General John Telelli, a three-star general at FORSCOM in Atlanta was made the point person on what kind of manpower and materials we would get for the Games.

We weren't making our relationships with the Army easy for them or us. I found out in February 1996 that while the military assumed that we would feed and transport the troops, that wasn't A. D. Frazier's understanding. With 165 days to go before the Games and having survived John McCain's temper tantrums, now we had an internal communications problem. Did we say we would feed and transport the military or not? A. D. said, no; I said, yes. The Army said we'll make it easy for you. Part of our request was money for bus drivers. The Army said we'll use that portion to feed our people and you can look elsewhere for drivers. We had enough problems with our transportation problems without losing 900 drivers. We got Nunn to help us put the military drivers back in the budget and, at the point we were about to announce that we were not going to run the Torch through Cobb County, we were also asking Gingrich to help us in the House. He did.

McCain had one last shot. In June 1996 with thirty-eight days to go before opening ceremonies, Senator Orrin Hatch held hearings on Olympic security and the Arizona senator was almost out of control. He took out his famous temper on General Telelli, an honorable man doing his duty. McCain couldn't get at us. Nunn had finessed him at every turn. So he turned his rage loose on General Telelli, who comported himself well and came out of that hearing looking more statesmanlike than did the senator.

Despite his temper tantrums, John McCain had almost no influence in the process thanks to Nunn, Coverdell, and others. He tried to embarrass us and intimidate us, but he was totally unsuccessful. After the bombing in Centennial Olympic Park, I tried in vain to get some of the national media to contact McCain to see if he had any comments, but to no avail.

On the state level, our principal contact was Governor Zell Miller. Again, we were in luck. Miller was a strong supporter of Bill Clinton and had nominated him for president at the Democratic Convention in 1992. He was known in some circles as "Clinton's favorite governor" and that was an accurate assessment. The strong relationship between the White House and the governor's office smoothed a lot of otherwise complicated relationships.

That didn't mean that we had a free ride in Georgia. If we missed the mark and had to ask for more money, it would be at the state level. The governor was leery of Billy Payne's enthusiasm and his penchant for overstatement, and not happy to read in the newspapers about "privately-funded" Games, knowing that we were in the process of presenting a number of proposals to the Georgia Legislature for state support.

In fact, the state was putting tax dollars into the Atlanta Games. They had agreed to spend $147 million to build new dormitories on the campus of Georgia Tech that would be used as housing for the athletes. We would contribute $47 million by leasing back the facilities from the state, and after the Games they would become student housing.

Unlike the City of Atlanta, state officials were well aware of the tremendous financial contributions that the Atlanta Games would make and the enormous exposure that would come as well. As a matter of fact, the "Atlanta" Games was a misnomer. While twenty-one events would be held inside the "Olympic Ring" an area some two and one-half miles across, an almost equal number would be outside the city. A number of venues such as softball, beach volleyball and yachting were located in other cities; preliminary rounds of soccer, in other states. Vice President Gore enjoyed referring to the Games as the "Ocoee Olympics" since the finals of that sport would be held on the Ocoee River in his home state of Tennessee.

University of Georgia economists estimated the impact on state's economy from the 1996 Games at $5.1 billion from both the thousands of jobs created and by the spending of Olympic visitors. But according to the study, the greatest legacy would be its potential to "'showcase' the state to the world." It was a lesson not lost on the governor and the General Assembly, but it seems to have gone right over the head of Atlanta's political leaders.

As any lobbyist can attest, no government body is "easy" to deal with and that included the state of Georgia. But over time, and with an excellent job by Lindsay Thomas in keeping the lines of communication open, and with strong support by management, we achieved legislation that tightened our ticket scalping laws, prevented hotels from price gouging, created a special license tag that brought much-needed revenue into our coffers, and agreed to handle its own overtime and housing costs.

We had one major issue with the state thanks to a little bug that almost resulted in moving one of the prime Olympic events, not only out of Georgia, but almost out of the country. There is a disease known as pyroplasmosis that affects horses, a kind of anemia. While horse owners in Europe treat the disease as no big deal, it is considered a serious issue in the United States. The Georgia Department of Agriculture said that no horse with the disease would be allowed into the state. To make matters worse, the head of the Equine Federation (FEI) was from Spain, home of IOC president Juan Antonio Samaranch. Samaranch was getting pressure to get the matter resolved; otherwise a number of Olympic-caliber horses wouldn't be coming to the states to compete. Samaranch was also making noises about moving the equine competition to another country, where the disease was treated more benignly than in the U.S. State Agriculture Commissioner Tommy Irvin is a powerful and astute politician, and was unmoved by Samaranch or anybody else, for that matter. Horse owners in the U.S. were waging a campaign to bar infected horses from the country. Rockdale County feared that after building the Georgia International Horse Park that it might be minus a few international horses there, not to mention an Olympic event. But Irvin was firm on not granting a waiver to allow horses with pyroplasmosis into the state.

Finally, a compromise was reached with all parties. We would construct—and pay for—a quarantine area for the horses to stay until it could be determined they were free of the disease. As I recall, one team from France was sent home.

Samaranch was happy. The FEI was happy. Commissioner Irvin was happy. We were out another million bucks or so, but relieved to get the issue resolved. No one asked the horses, but I assume they were happy, too.

Governor Miller began to relax as he saw progress instead of rhetoric. At one time or the other, Payne, Frazier, Thomas, and I had been, individually and collectively, the recipients of his displeasure and it was an experience one could do without. But Miller was determined that we would not embarrass the State of Georgia and we did not. As with Mack McLarty at the White House and Sam Nunn in the United States Senate, I don't know how we would have made it without Zell Miller.

When the curtain fell on the evening of August 4 and the 1996 Centennial Olympic Games were over, it was time for reflection. I remembered the term, "government works" which is a euphemism for welfare programs and government boondoggles. But in my mind, "government works" means what it says. The federal government and the State of Georgia—despite all of the disputes and disagreements and the posturing with each other over the past four years—had worked magnificently.

# 7

## NO GOOD DEED
## GOES UNPUNISHED

*We are easy pickings for anybody that wants to take a shot at us.*
—Diary Entry, July 20, 1995

No good deed goes unpunished. Particularly, if that deed is the Olympic Games. The 1996 Centennial Olympic Games attracted special interest groups as a light bulb draws moths. I would have to kill half the trees in the forest to recount all the groups—some serious, some absurd—that tried to use us as a megaphone for their special cause as we made our way through the planning process. Whatever their interest, they all used the same tactic—threats. We were threatened by the unions, poor people, rich people, the disabled, anti-alcohol groups, pro-state flag groups, animal rights activists, preachers, Hispanics, Native Americans, blacks, whites, feminists, gays, environmentalists, neighborhoods, cities, counties. You name it. Everybody wanted a piece of us.

We angered a University of Georgia professor in an effort to rescue the image of our woebegone mascot, Whatizit. We had asked a group of twelve-year-olds to give the creature a name. The mascot, which had been referred to as *The Blob* and "a sperm with legs," wasn't a big hit with the public, to understate things a bit, and had provided our resident aesthete and local columnist, Colin Campbell, with reams of copy about which to harrumph. We figured to position our cute little liability as "being for children. If you aren't a child, you won't understand him." There was an element of truth to the statement. Mascot dolls sold like hot cakes to children. The kids liked him and were delighted with the opportunity to name him. We convened a panel of young people who after some deliberation, named him Izzy. We were pleased with the results and promptly registered the name. The UGA professor was not pleased. He found the name a slur on Jewish people and complained to the Anti-Defamation League. There was some momentary concern that we would find the ADL marching around our building and chanting, "Ho. Ho. Izzy Must Go." Less far-fetched things had happened. But to the ADL's credit, they issued a statement that said not only was Izzy not anti-Semitic, but they had more important things to deal with than this. End of issue.

One particular protest group—the Women's Sports Foundation—used kids to try and advance a charge that we were insensitive to women's athletics. I am not sure even today what they thought they would accomplish. I am extremely proud of the role women athletes played in the 1996 Games. More women would complete in Atlanta than in any other Games, 20% more women athletes than were in Barcelona four years earlier. We added thirteen new sports for women. My favorite statistic was that we sold more tickets to women's sports (3.9 million) than Barcelona had sold tickets for all sports—men and women—combined (3.7 million).

This seemed of little import to the Women's Sports Foundation. They had a much bigger issue. They did not like our pictograms. These are the symbols used to designate individual Olympic sports pictorially. They had complained in early 1994 that our pictograms must be viewed "as universal interpretations of the human form." What made this issue bizarre to me was that the forms we were using were representations of figures that had adorned Greek vases in ancient times. Frankly, I couldn't tell the difference. Still, we tweaked the figures, hoping to satisfy the group. Of course, it didn't.

The Foundation interviewed third grade through seventh grade kids about the pictograms. More than half the kids thought the women's pictograms looked like women and the men looked like men. The remainder thought the pictograms looked like either male or female. This information indicated that most of the youngsters agreed with us. The women's group didn't see it that way. They called it overwhelming evidence of the sexist nature of the pictograms. They wanted an apology, an admission that we were wrong, to call NBC and tell them not to use the pictograms, then they would let us off the hook. To make sure we understood our sins clearly, the Foundation added, "To the extent that women athletes are being left out of the picture by the ACOG pictogram program, they are being symbolically reduced to second-class citizens in Olympic sports." Forget the thirteen new sports for women, the number of tickets sold to women's events, and the astonishing performance of the women in Atlanta. Rather than celebrate the enormous progress that the Centennial Games would bring to women's athletics in closing a too-real gender equity gap, they chose to raise hell about amorphous Greek figures that even a group of prepubescent children had a hard time making sexist. No wonder political correctness has such a bad name.

We received hundreds of letters and petitions from anti-alcohol groups upset about Anheuser-Busch being an Olympic sponsor. The Hispanic Chamber of Commerce thought we weren't spending enough money with their members. Environmentalists were convinced that we would single-handedly kill off the wood stork with our yachting venue off the Georgia coast, and even if we didn't, we would give lead poisoning to every other living thing at our skeet-shooting venue at Wolf Creek. (Finally, we did neither.) Animal rights activists wanted to be sure that we didn't release live doves during opening ceremonies. In the 1988 Games in Seoul, Korea, most of the doves had flown onto the cauldron and perched, just in time to be barbecued by the lighting of the Olympic flame. I knew we were finally in the big leagues when Jesse Jackson showed up one day with some kind of union-poor peoples coalition and stomped around in our lobby as everybody sang songs and blocked elevators.

Dealing with protests was the hardest and most debilitating part of my job for several reasons. First, you have to gauge the potential damage that an individual or group can inflict on an organization. At BellSouth, we hoped to be around for a while so we took a long-range perspective in external decisions. Time was a luxury we did not have at ACOG. Second, you have to decide if you are willing to stand up to the pressure special interest groups can bring to bear. If not, you must decide what you are willing to give up in terms of money, time, operating control, etc., in order to get out from under that pressure. You also have to deal with the internal management reactions to the demands of special interest groups. Nobody wants to be told they can't do business as they choose and they particularly don't want to hear it from a mean-spirited crowd that doesn't give a whit about your business, only theirs. Explaining this to management can make you look disloyal and not a team player. Finally, there is the ancient Olympic sport of second-guessing by the media. They enjoy standing on the sidelines watching you squirm, secretly gratified that they don't have to make those tough decisions themselves. (Sad to say, but that I have become a newspaper columnist, I am prone to do the same thing.)

The temptation is to tell the agitators to "go to hell." Sometimes that is the right answer; sometimes it isn't. The trick is to know the difference. For example, we had a black preacher who didn't like the fact that we had selected a local radio station, WGST, as our "official" station, meaning that for a fee, we would allow them to broadcast from our facilities during the Games. WGST, like many radio stations, was an all-talk format, very conservative, highly opinionated and perceived by some in the black community as racist. The preacher was threatening a boycott if we didn't renounce our relationship with the station. He dropped a lot of names of people who were going to help him.

He did offer us a way out. If we would apologize, pay him $6,500 to cover the costs he had put into his effort, he would go away. If cash was a problem, he had a Plan B. We could run one $300 ad each week in a publication he produced.

Shirley Franklin is as plugged into the community as anybody in town. She did some discreet checking and learned that even among the black clergy, nobody knew the guy. That was a surprise because he wasn't a young man. We decided to call his bluff. We just didn't have the time or the resources to combat his threat. It was a risk, but it worked — we never heard from him again.

Nor did we hear again from a group of inner city ministers who demanded we set up a $3 million trust fund and interest free loans, and made the usual threats if we didn't. This was to cover the monies they claimed they would forego from collections since the Games would occur over three successive Sundays. It was their studied opinion that members would be unable to come to church during those three Sundays because of the crowds, thus our "contribution." An incredulous Billy Payne asked them first if they had ever heard of the U.S. Mail, and then basically told them to get lost. I assume somehow these churches managed to survive financially, although I am surprised they didn't make a bigger scene than they did. I can only guess that it was so close to opening ceremonies and everybody was so tired, planners and protesters alike, that their heart wasn't in it.

Of all the special-interest battles we fought, there were three issues that preoccupied the management at the Atlanta Committee during the years leading up to the Games. They were handicap access to our facilities, gay rights, and the Georgia State flag. Each played out differently, but all had two things in common—there were strong feelings on both sides and we took them all very, very seriously.

Our management of external issues was understandably convoluted, given that we were a temporary organization basically making things up as we went along. There was not much of a template to follow, especially in the United States where we have raised protests to an art form. That is the price of democracy, and it is a small one, although I sometimes had a hard time keeping that civics lesson in mind. I was responsible for federal and state relations, and my colleague Shirley Franklin for the city and county governments and the special interest groups. Needless to say, we worked closely together.

The disabled community suffered discrimination far too long in their efforts to become a functioning part of society. It wasn't until the passage of the Americans with Disabilities Act (ADA) in 1990 that the disabled leveled the playing field. That sweeping law required that new construction, alterations or renovations to existing buildings and facilities of both private companies and state and local governments be made accessible to persons with disabilities. It also included communications and "reasonable modifications" of policies and practices that may be discriminatory. It also gave the Department of Justice, specifically, the Civil Rights Division, authority for enforcement.

Congress in its infinite wisdom managed somehow to exclude the federal government from the Act. I found it ironic that on our frequent visits to the Department of Justice to negotiate the ADA requirements at the Atlanta Games, we walked up the steps to the building, passing a sheet of plywood that had been placed on the steps. That was their handicapped access entry. It just proved that some—like the federal government—are more equal than others.

Before I arrived at ACOG, the organization had established a number of advisory groups: Disabled, Environment, Cultural, Medical, External, etc. One of my first acts was to disband the external advisory group. I had enough problems without a lot of second-guessing from people who didn't have to assume final responsibility for their decision. Besides, I had the media to do that.

We later terminated the environmental group, much to the howling of the members and the media. We asked for an environmental plan and had received it, but some members seemed to think they had pointed out enough environmental issues that we would have to hire them to help save the day. Much to their consternation, this didn't happen.

The advisory group for the disabled was adversarial, to put it mildly. Known as the Committee on Disabled Access (CODA), they had started their relationship with us by a loud confrontational demonstration in our lobby. They wouldn't be easy to deal with. I didn't blame them. I can't imagine being sightless or unable to drive my car or powerless to walk up a flight of stairs unaided. Those are everyday challenges to the disabled. They chafe at what they consider favored treatment for other groups that have known discrimination. The disabled regard themselves as victims without the same rights. They are also politically astute. The ADA gave them leverage and they applied it with all their might. Had I been handicapped, I no doubt would have felt the same way. But I was not being paid to be empathetic. I was hired to manage the external environment, which included dealing with the Department of Justice.

I had my work cut out for me. The Civil Rights Division early on placed three conditions on our new stadium. None of the conditions impacted the Games. Rather, they were fixes that had to do with the stadium's afterlife as a baseball facility. They wanted more handicapped seating in the club level, more access to the restaurants and handicapped access to the dugouts. Since we were building the stadium, the solutions to these issues would have to come before it was finished. Our job wasn't made any easier, in my opinion, in that the attorney in the Department of Justice handling the negotiations was himself handicapped. I realized quickly how the game would be played.

In December 1993, we received a letter from Department of Justice threatening us with a lawsuit if we did not agree to their stipulations on the stadium by the end of the year, just a few weeks away. Our tight construction schedule and an even tighter budget couldn't take delays and major design changes and we certainly couldn't make those important decisions in a week or two. To make matters worse, this supposedly private document was immediately leaked to the newspapers.

If our friends in the disabled community could do an end around, so could we. We let it be known in the political arena that if we were sued by the Department of Justice for issues not related to the Olympic Games—such as making the baseball dugouts handicapped accessible—with no chance to negotiate, we felt the general public would be very critical of the federal government in general and the Clinton administration specifically. With that, we received assurances from the attorneys who had written the letter that they really didn't mean they were going to sue us immediately. They were just trying to get our attention. After our end-runs around each other, we clearly had each other's attention. The disabled leaders screamed as loud at our move as we had at the leak to the newspaper.

Our own insensitivity to the disabled community didn't help us. At a meeting of CODA in early January 1994, we laid out a carefully prepared agenda as the basis for the meeting. The only problem was that one of the members was blind and we had made no provisions for Braille. Frankly, I was as offended as they were.

One of the issues the group pushed was a special assistant who was disabled to report directly to Billy Payne. This was nothing new. Every special interest group wanted a representative to report to him. Billy patiently pointed out to them on a number of occasions that Shirley Franklin was their advocate and was a direct report. That didn't mollify them. But when they questioned Shirley's enthusiasm for their cause, they overstepped their bounds. She angrily accused them of a racist, anti-feminist attitude. End of complaint.

Dr. Jim Cherry headed the CODA group. Himself disabled, his job was made more difficult by the fact that he couldn't speak for all of his members. Like any politically motivated group, there were hard-liners and compromisers, but in CODA, I found more of the former, than the latter.

We wrestled with the issue for all of 1994 and into 1995. The Justice Department's attorney was turning up the heat, wanting information on our ticket plans, our seating arrangements, all of our other venue plans, a thousand other details and pushing for a consent order. In late-1995, with less than 300 days to go before opening ceremonies, we were again threatened with a lawsuit. I don't think the Clinton administration wanted to be put in that position of suing us, when we believed we had made a good faith effort at complying with the ADA, only to have the civil rights attorneys continue to raise the bar higher and higher. By now, we were considering suing the federal government.

You reach a point in disputes like this that your only weapon is to take the issue public. Get ahead of the other side and hope you win in the court of public opinion. That is hard to do in a corporation like BellSouth, because the public isn't too keen on big corporations. The Olympic Games is a different story, particularly if it looks like the government—loved even less than big business—is being unreasonable. The pressure was building on both sides.

Enter Duvall Patrick, assistant attorney general in charge of the Civil Rights Division of the Department of Justice. Patrick was not what one would expect the head of the civil rights division to be. He was a helluva nice guy, a bright young African-American who didn't seem to be pursuing any personal agenda. He was very likable and in a delicious irony not lost on him, inhabited J. Edgar Hoover's old office. He laughed about what the former FBI head would think if he knew that a black man was occupying his office. I would kid him about not saying that too loud—Hoover's ghost might be lurking somewhere in the building.

Patrick found himself caught in the middle between a hard-line defense of an important constituency and the hard political realities of a lawsuit. He wanted out of the mess his attorneys, the disabled community, and ACOG had put him in. The best way to do it was to drop the posturing and start talking and keep talking until we reached common ground. The good news is that as chaotic as our committee was, we were all pulling together on this issue. Kay Wallace, the assistant chief operating officer who reported to A. D. Frazier, was representing the operating departments and able to tell us what was reasonable and what was not in terms of changes and budgets. Horace Sibley, one of the original members of the volunteer team with assistance from our outside counsel, Marva Brooks, a former city of Atlanta attorney, and Josie Alexander, a prominent local civil right attorney, were working hard to find middle ground with the Justice Department. Unlike many issues we dealt with, everybody was talking to everybody and looking for solutions.

Duvall Patrick went out of his way to keep his attorneys focused on a solution, not a public relations victory. It didn't look possible but he made us keep talking. Finally, Sibley and the Justice Department attorneys got an agreement.

It was a very benign agreement under the circumstance. We made many of the changes that the Department of Justice had demanded. The tone of the agreement was neither accusatory nor punitive. All in all, it was a great relief to get the issue behind us. To the credit of the disabled community, they accepted the terms, even if a little reluctant to do so. They had fought the good fight and in the end, I think we all—the disabled, the Department of Justice, and ACOG—could claim some little victory. That meant it was a good compromise and we all had Duvall Patrick to thank for keeping all the players focused on doing the right thing. I just wished our local politicians could have been that responsible.

The interesting thing about our battles with the disabled community is that they never received much splash in the media. Not as much as they could have. Perhaps that was because the biggest external fight during my tenure at ACOG dwarfed all the other issues. It was a gay rights battle in Cobb County, dubbed Olympics Out of Cobb, which is exactly what the gay rights groups were advocating and Hollywood could not have cast a better set of characters for the drama: the powerful Newt Gingrich, Speaker of the U.S. House of Representatives, the arch-conservative Cobb County Commission, and its hard-nosed chairman, Bill Byrne, Olympic gold medallist diver, Greg Louganis, gay rights activists, local churches claiming to be the official spokespersons for God, the Coca-Cola Company, the Atlanta Committee for the Olympic Games, the state of Georgia, members of Congress, and worldwide media, to name a few. Unlike most issues we dealt with at ACOG, this one split the management and had the local newspaper direly predicting that however the matter was decided internally, the "losers" in the battle would resign from the committee. Like many of their other dire predictions, that never happened, of course.

Cobb is an affluent county northwest of the city of Atlanta. Its 500,000 residents are mostly white, largely conservative, and a large number live in upper-middle-class suburbs, including me.

We had announced that we would hold preliminary volleyball competitions at Cobb Galleria Centre, the county's new $48 million convention center. It wasn't our first effort to bring an Olympic event to Cobb County. We had proposed women's fast pitch softball, but that had fallen through when voters rejected a bond referendum to upgrade the facility for the event. Some thought the preliminary volleyball venue a "consolation prize." But most welcomed the event.

Four months earlier in August 1993, the Cobb County Commission had passed a resolution extolling "family virtues." Not something that would normally get people's hackles up but there was more to this resolution. It had been passed, the commissioners claimed, in response to a domestic partnership ordinance that had been enacted by the Atlanta City Council, extending employee benefits to "live-in" domestic partners, including gay couples.

If the movement spread to other governmental agencies, the Cobb commissioners said, the consequences could mean tax increases for its constituents. Just to be sure everyone understood the even-handedness of their concern, the resolution added, "Lifestyles advocated by the gay community are incompatible with the standards to which this community subscribes." Chairman Byrne quickly added that the resolution, which had no legal standing, was not intended as an attack on gays, just on the issue of adding employee benefits for same sex unions. However, the resolution's author, Gordon Wysong, said, "I felt it was important that we were not going to spend our money to implement the gay agenda." At the same time, the commissioners refused funding to the local Theatre in the Square, which had presented "Lips Together, Teeth Apart," a show that included some references to homosexuality.

Call me naïve, but I believe the Cobb Commission — taxpayers' interests notwithstanding — thought they had found a politically attractive issue that would catch on statewide and put them in the vanguard of that issue. That is how political careers are born. Wysong bragged that the commission had received between 8,000 and 9,000 phone calls and "80 to 90 percent [of the calls were] supportive." An *Atlanta Journal-Constitution* poll found only 33% of Cobb residents backed the resolution. In addition, the Atlanta ordinance was later declared unconstitutional in Fulton County Superior Court, but that was of little import to Byrne and Wysong.

They had greatly miscalculated their support, and the explosive reaction that followed would put Cobb County in the world's spotlight and us on the hot seat. Lines were drawn and were attracting some very powerful interests on both sides. As if things weren't difficult enough already, in the middle of the fight, I was diagnosed with prostate cancer and would need surgery. It was not a fun time.

The controversy had a benign start. On January 30, 1994, Atlanta was celebrating another big event. Super Bowl XXVIII was in town. To the

NFL, the Super Bowl is the ultimate sporting spectacular. To those of us involved in planning for the Olympic Games, it was just a warm-up for what was to come but it had a useful purpose for us. NBC, as a part of our agreement with them, was running the first of a number of Olympic specials on the Centennial Games. The initial program aired just before the pre-game Super Bowl festivities and we felt it would be a great way to remind people that the Olympic Games were coming to Atlanta in just two and a half years.

In the show, we urged the network to emphasize that a number of cities and counties in Georgia would be participating in the Centennial Olympics, not just the city of Atlanta. We wanted to be sure that any state officials watching television would be pleased and favorably inclined to help us move future legislation. The term "Atlanta" doesn't bring smiles to many of our state legislators who view their capital city with the same warm regard they have for New York City.

One of the counties spotlighted as an Olympic venue that night was Cobb County, home of both preliminary volleyball, and the anti-gay resolution. As I proudly watched the NBC program in my office with my wife, son, and daughter-in-law before heading over to the Georgia Dome for the game, a gay named Jon Ivan Weaver, a silk-screen designer, was watching the same show in horror. He couldn't believe his eyes. The Olympic Games were holding an event in a location where gays clearly would not be welcomed.

Whatever one may think of gay people and the gay rights movement, give them credit for their ability to organize. The Cobb County commission had handed them a made-to-order issue and the Atlanta Committee for the Olympic Games would provide the stage. I had to agree with the Cobb County sheriff who said, "Why stir up those people? Hardly anyone knows they're here."

The first major protest occurred a month later in downtown Atlanta. The march attracted some seventy people and the event was peaceful. Speakers denounced the county, naturally, and encouraged us to move the venue. My antenna went up when I saw the march, small by protest standards, displayed prominently in the *Atlanta Journal-Constitution* with two color photos of the marchers. Not a good sign.

Our first strategy was to stick to our guns that we were not in the business of "politics." We would leave that to the county. We were about "putting on the Games." That wouldn't fly with the gay rights group.

Besides, hadn't we pulled golf out of Augusta because of the protests of black politicians? Hadn't Jimmy Carter refused to let our athletes compete in the 1980 Moscow Olympics because of the Soviet Union's human rights record? The matter was totally political.

The county showed no contrition and no interest in rescinding the resolution. We began to search for allies who could persuade the commission to find some area of compromise. By this time, Chairman Byrne had pretty much taken the issue away from Wysong and was handling things himself.

I have been around a lot of politicians over my career, but Bill Byrne may have been the most "unpolitical" I ever met. A former Marine who wears a Marine Corps lapel pin about the size of a Volkswagen hubcap, he has been an effective chairman. The county is prosperous and the political scandals minimal. He seems to care little about positive press, which is a good thing because he doesn't get much. He is also very direct. When the Cobb Chamber of Commerce became concerned that pressure might cause us to move the venue, he called their concerns "garbage." When we mused publicly about whether we could stay in Cobb, given the resolution, the chairman said we could "take it or leave it" but he wasn't going to rescind it. Besides, Byrne said, gays should not feel unwelcome in Cobb. He emphasized that point by adding that all law-abiding groups were welcomed, including "Nazis and skinheads."

When it became apparent that the issue wasn't going to be resolved quickly or easily, I went to see the chairman to see if we could find some area of compromise. I had never met him and found him gracious and non-defensive about the issue. His decision had been financially and politically motivated. The cost of a domestic partnership benefits program would be prohibitive to the county, he said. Byrne said much of what is wrong with society came from a reduced emphasis on family. He told me that he held no animosity toward gays, just their life style. "After all," he said, "my daughter is gay." I almost fell out of my chair. Some months later, his daughter, Shannon, did announce she was gay and denounced her father for voting for the resolution.

I suggested a new resolution that was more welcoming—minus the skinheads and Nazis—and he thought that a good idea but warned me the issue wouldn't go away. He was right.

The issue continued to escalate. I didn't help matters by poorly preparing Billy Payne for an editorial board meeting with the *Atlanta*

*Journal-Constitution*. As a public relations practitioner, I don't believe in spontaneity. I've always been adept at guessing what questions the media were going to ask and coming up with short, understandable answers. When Billy was hospitalized with cardiac problems, we asked his surgeon to hold a news conference on Billy's condition prior to the surgery. I gave him a list of eight questions I thought he would be asked and some suggestions as to answers. He was asked all eight and responded beautifully. When the media left, we both agreed that he should stick to heart surgery and I should be doing what I do for a living and we promised to never get in the other's business.

That wasn't the case in the interview at the paper. Billy was asked about why we didn't pull the venue out of Cobb County because of the prejudice against gays. He said, "I don't believe there is an analogy between African Americans who are minorities legally and given protection and gays and lesbians who have not yet attained that legal status." Not a good answer and it was my fault. It was more ammunition for those wanting us to get out of Cobb County.

As the heat began to build, Byrne seemed more and more amenable to a compromise. The Olympics Out of Cobb group wanted a full surrender—rescind the old resolution. The commission wasn't willing to do that but they were willing to issue a new one that extolled the virtues of "human rights" and that their concern was the "domestic partnership concept." The county was taking a pounding around the world. To the chagrin of the business leaders, Cobb County was being portrayed as a redneck, backward, and unprogressive place to live and work.

I thought Newt Gingrich might understand that and help us convince the commission to seek some common ground with the gay rights groups. While Weaver and his group were getting the most publicity—and loving it—the substantive work was being done by the Cobb Citizens Coalition, a group of gay rights and community activists who had more political savvy than the Olympics Out of Cobb group. I thought things were beginning to fall in place for a satisfactory conclusion to the issue.

Gingrich was in town to make a speech at the downtown Commerce Club to a group of his donors. Lobbyist Cindy Gillespie arranged a few minutes for me to brief him on the situation and to see what kind of advice he might have for me. Before I could begin my spiel, I was ripped by the Speaker for "caving in." He was extremely critical of the

International Olympic Committee for their earlier decision to drop South Africa from the Games because of their apartheid policies and yet allow countries like the Soviet Union and China who had terrible human rights records to continue to participate. He thought the whole thing was hypocritical. With the dressing down completed, he left me standing somewhat dazed as he went into the dining room to great applause from his loyalists.

Just when you think politicians blow with the prevailing winds of public opinion, one comes along and bucks the trend. Johnny Isakson, a state senator from Cobb County and a former gubernatorial candidate, recognized the damage to the county's image. He and some of his colleagues, including Chuck Clay, another senator from Cobb County and grandson of World War II hero General Lucius Clay, and Matt Towery, a state representative who had been Isakson's running mate as Lt. Governor, were working with the commission, the business community, and ACOG for some solution that would keep the venue in Cobb County. Isakson publicly called the original resolution a "mistake," and said rescinding it "would be the best thing they could possibly do." He acknowledged that wouldn't happen, but he urged all sides to accept a milder resolution and stop the battle. With the powerful conservative churches in Cobb strongly pushing the resolution, going public took a lot of guts on Isakson's part, but he is one of those rare politicians—Sam Nunn was another—who has shown the good side of politics by taking principled stands and leaving the posturing to others. They always seem to be above the political fray. When Gingrich flamed out and retired from Congress, he was replaced by Johnny Isakson. I predict he will be a person of great influence in that body, as he has been in Georgia and Cobb County.

Certainly, bucking the churches was risky. The large majority of the churches strongly backed the county's anti-gay stance. Some 270 conservative church leaders had held a rally to let the commission know of their support for the resolution. A much smaller group of thirty-seven religious leaders in the county came to our defense. They included Jewish synagogues, Episcopalians, Congregationalists, and Catholics—all who have a reputation for supporting liberal issues. Also, there was one Presbyterian and three Methodist churches on the list.

My wise father once told me never to argue politics or religion because you won't win either argument. However, I was amazed at how vile, vulgar, and downright threatening people were in the Name of the Lord. For a religion that espouses love and forgiveness, I found scant little of either in the ranting and raving of my supposedly Christian brethren, including the preachers who, while in the pulpit, denounced us. If what I heard and read and saw during the Cobb County battle is indicative, the Christian Right (I found them neither "Christian" nor "right") has more to worry about than gays and volleyball. The first place to start is by looking in the mirror. The churches were sadly lacking leadership in the Cobb County episode.

While the external battles raged, the issue was getting hot inside the organization as well. A. D. Frazier was adamant about holding the line. Our finances were tenuous to say the least. Moving the venue would cost us $4 million that we didn't have in mid-1994. Frazier was good to let me do my job and not interfere. Besides, he had more than enough on his plate to keep him busy. On moving out of Cobb, however, he was hard-line. Not only would that be expensive, but it would play havoc with logistics. Where would the athletes stay? How do you transport them? What about tickets? What about negotiations with a new facility? How much would that cost? Last, but not least, was the fact that the International Volleyball Federation was headed by Rueben Acosta, of Brazil, a powerful member of the Olympics family, and any move of the venue would require his approval and probably some huge concessions on our part. None of this did A. D. need at this particular time. Frazier wanted the Galleria complex, which was not a part of the Cobb County government, to include a paragraph in the contract saying they would not discriminate. I disagreed. The Galleria wasn't the issue. The Cobb County Commission was the issue. Unless the resolution was rescinded, the gay-rights groups were going to continue to apply pressure. Our disagreement was beginning to show in our relationship. I have described our talks as "pleasantly contentious." In addition, we were both lobbying Billy Payne who, as CEO, would have to make the final decision. And we were both trying separately to convince ACOG cochairman Bob Holder of our point of view. A. D.'s argument, beyond the expense and the horrendous logistical issues a move would bring, was that we were inviting every other special interest group to pressure us for their benefit. Holder agreed we should hold the line until we saw the language in the proposed Galleria contract and whether or not it would be accepted. If not, then he favored moving it.

The paper picked up on the dispute which was being rumored around the offices and a column appeared on a Saturday in early April that the Cobb issue was a "power struggle" between A. D. Frazier and me, and cast A. D. as being recalcitrant, and me as the person urging the move out of Cobb. It was upsetting because it looked like I had planted the article to put pressure on him. That isn't my style. Frazier and I had a number of disagreements but they were face-to-face. I wasn't going to go behind his back. To A. D.'s credit, he believed me when I called him at home to tell him.

No matter what we hoped, the issue was not going to go away in Cobb County. By April, we were still intending to keep the venue in the county and saying so to the world. At the same time, the gay community was getting better organized and bolder. When we unveiled the cauldron design at a media conference in March, two Olympics Out of Cobb members, posing as members of the media, talked their way into the meeting. As festivities commenced, these two members unfurled their Olympics Out of Cobb banner to the shock of everybody in the room. I ran up and snatched the banner out of their hands and had Scott Mall, a pugnacious member of my staff escort them downstairs along with our security personnel. I figured if anyone could keep them from coming back, Scott could. Interestingly, the incident got little play in the media. No one followed the demonstrators out to interview them. But they had made their point.

The issue was getting hotter. Every morning when I got to work, I would have some fifteen to twenty voice mails sent during the night. Half of them accused me of siding with the gays; the other half thought I was in Cobb County's pocket. I remember one particular call when I was accused of being a right-wing sympathizer. The caller left his number and dared me to call him. On this particular day, I happened to get in about 4:30 AM. I returned his call immediately. He was so shocked at being awakened at that time of the morning that he had lost some of his ardor for the issue. I guess he just wanted to go back to sleep. Some people are more passionate about their beliefs than others.

While maintaining their focus on us, the gay rights movement began to pressure Coca-Cola, the largest and most prominent of the Olympic sponsors. Coke officials were told by a national gay rights group that if the issue was not resolved in a week, they would call for a nationwide boycott of Coca-Cola products. Greg Louganis, a three time Olympic gold medallist, and one of the most respected figures in sports who himself was gay, publicly criticized our continued efforts to stay with the Cobb County site.

The Commission had issued a second resolution in April, softening their anti-gay stance but had no intention of rescinding the original resolution. Shirley Franklin continued to work the gay rights groups as I was working the Cobb side. We again came close to an agreement. So close, in fact, that I received word from the commission and the Cobb Citizens Coalition on a Friday night in mid-May that a compromise had been reached. I gave reporters my beeper number to call me on Saturday for a reaction. By noon, Saturday no one had called me so I began to call around to see what had happened. It wasn't good. As the coalition members walked into Byrne's office on Saturday morning fully expecting to sign a deal that would satisfy them and keep the venue in Cobb, Byrne suggested they not sit down because the deal was off.

What happened? The chairman and the local daily in Marietta have no love for each other. In the midst of seeking a compromise, Byrne had taken time to throw out the first pitch at an Atlanta Braves baseball game. He was roundly booed. That gave the *Marietta Daily Journal* the opportunity to editorialize about the lack of popularity for the "family values" resolution. The *Marietta Daily Journal* had opposed it all along because of the damage it was doing to the county's image.

The editorial told the chairman that baseball fans drive pickup trucks and drink beer and they don't like you either. These were supposedly the very people the commission thought would be solidly behind their resolution. That was more than Byrne could take. He called the meeting off before it could get started, blasted the paper for "fostering an atmosphere that ruled out compromise," stuck out his hand to the startled coalition members and said, "Thanks for coming." It was time to get the hell out of Cobb.

Earlier, I had given Billy—at his request—a strategy paper on our alternatives, which included riding out the storm or packing it up and leaving. The commission was making it easy for us. By early June, Billy was convinced that it was time to go. We had a commission that was too emotionally tied to this harmful resolution to admit a mistake or, as one of the members said, the board might come off "looking weak" if they did. "As far as I am concerned," the commissioner member added, "the board is willing to live with the resolution and take the lumps." That is called cutting off your nose to spite your face.

There was one more effort to get another resolution passed, but it came to naught. Then Byrne beat us to the punch by asking us to either commit to the county or leave. On July 29, six months after the initial controversy, we moved the preliminary volleyball venue to the University of Georgia. I called Bill Byrne and told him the news and he was gracious and wished us the best. I also counseled Billy that he should tell Gingrich, since the Speaker deserved to hear from the CEO. I volunteered to call Bob Barr, who also represents Cobb and is the most conservative member of the Georgia delegation. Barr's reaction was not what I expected. "Dick," he said, "of course, I don't agree with what you are doing, but I understand why you did it. I am not going to publicly congratulate you on your decision, but I won't attack you either." That was a relief. Barr, as the Clinton impeachment team was to find out later, can be very hard-line when he chooses. He wasn't going to make it an issue.

As I finished the conversation, Billy came into my office looking like a deer staring into headlights. Gingrich, in Billy's words, had "gone ballistic." It isn't wise to have the third most powerful public figure in the land mad at you. My counsel to my CEO, for what its worth, was to forget it. Newt Gingrich was famous for his explosions (as I had found out at the Commerce Club luncheon), but he could not put himself in a position not to help us. His positive ratings with the American public were never high anyway, and if he came out opposing the Olympic Games in his home state, he would give the Clinton administration and the national and local media a wonderful issue with which to beat him up. He would look petty and small-minded and wasn't so popular at home that he could afford that kind of perception. The Speaker was to be enraged with us later when we announced we would not run the torch through Cobb County, but he got over his pique and was a great help to us for the duration.

Today, Bill Byrne remains chairman of Cobb County. Gordon Wysong won one reelection and lost the next. The volleyball venue was a big success at the University of Georgia. I had my cancer surgery as soon as the Cobb issue was settled, and of this writing I have had no further problems.

As I think back on the furor that a preliminary round of volleyball caused us, I can only think that "never have so many done so much for so little."

Both the handicapped access issue and the Cobb County flap had to be handled before the Games began. There was no choice because they both directly involved our ability to put on the Games. The third issue wouldn't physically prevent us from staging the Games, but it threatened to be a high profile issue right through the end. It was the Georgia state flag.

In 1956, the Georgia legislature had replaced the existing state flag with one that featured the Confederate Stars and Bars. I don't think half the people in the state even knew what the flag looked like until Zell Miller assumed the governor's office. In his first legislative session in 1993, he proposed to change the flag back to the pre-1956 version. The reaction was immediate and polarizing. The flag was a racist symbol to some and a tribute to Southern heritage to others. The local paper, in the form of Colin Campbell, took up the challenge of supporting Miller's stance. Campbell was totally ignored. The pro-state flag groups prevailed and Miller, realizing he had stepped into a no-win situation, backed off and moved on to other more important issues like improving the quality of education in the state. But the issue refused to go away, and both sides tried to draw us into the debate. Would we fly the Georgia flag at the Centennial Games or would we not? If we did, we would be offending a large constituency who found the flag racist. We would also run the risk of a boycott by athletes opposed to the flag. Our contract with NBC stated that if any of the twelve top medal-winning countries in 1992 failed to show, the network could renegotiate the contract and that could cost us big bucks. Since many of the top athletes at the summer games are African or African American, the risk of a boycott was possible, if not probable. On the other hand, if we said we were not going to fly the state flag, we would no doubt offend the legislature and risk losing much of the support we needed from them.

We were working protesters overtime. Those who opposed gay rights seemed to be solidly behind flying the Georgia state flag. As far as they were concerned, we had more than justified our reputation as godless commies. The anti-flag crowd was pro-gay rights and convinced we were all still a bunch of neo-Nazi rednecks.

What neither side knew or cared was that the Olympic Charter was specific on the matter of flags. We would fly the U.S. flag, the Olympic flag, and the flags of nations competing in the Games. There was no provision to fly the Georgia flag, even if we wanted to. But what good is a controversy if it is confused with facts? Both sides continued to hammer us on the issue and we stood our ground. It got terribly confusing for them where we were renting state facilities. The decision of whether or not the state flag would fly on state property wasn't ours to make. I think even the dumbest protesters understood that fact.

There was nothing left for the pro-flag crowd to do but to embarrass us before the world's television audience. We were being told that people would be bringing state flags into the venues and wearing tee shirts with the Georgia flag emblazoned across the front. Once again, we didn't help the situation by printing on the back of our tickets that among the items that would be prohibited in the stadium—along with noise makers, coolers, etc.—were any flags other than "national flags." It wasn't putting that condition on the ticket that was the gaffe. It was the fact that it was done without consulting any one. Of course, it caused an uproar. Our attorney general, Michael Bowers, was a Republican gearing up to run for governor. He questioned the constitutionality of the flag prohibition and made it clear he would not prosecute anyone who we did stop. I could almost hear the media jumping up and down with glee at the ugly spectacle about to unfold.

I would have bet, as would everyone else at ACOG, that the flag controversy would surface many times over the course of the Games. We would just have to deal with the incidents as they arose.

As it turned out, we had only one flag incident. A Taiwanese waved the flag of Taiwan in front of a group of Republic of China athletes performing at the Georgia Dome. He was evicted.

After all the earlier threats, there were no state flag incidents on either side of the issue. I don't know why, but I have a theory. I believe the Olympic Games were so exciting, so much fun and so unifying that nobody could get up enough selfishness and meanness to raise hell.

Besides, they had raised more than enough hell for the previous five years.

# 8

## A BLOWN OPPORTUNITY:
## THE SAD STREETS OF ATLANTA

*The mayor probably won't care but he has tagged the city for years to come.*
— Diary Entry, August 4, 1996

The City of Atlanta Government blew the Games—pure and simple. What could have been an opportunity to show the world we were the major league city we claim to be was instead an embarrassing display of tacky shacks blocking sidewalks and impeding traffic flow. We should have seen it coming. From the beginning, negotiations were contentious and full of racial threats.

I had been with the Atlanta Committee for the Olympic Games only a few days when Billy invited me to a meeting with A. D. Frazier at City Hall to discuss marketing issues with Mayor Maynard Jackson and some of his staff members. The city's marketing director was Joel Babbitt, a well-known *enfant terrible* in the local advertising community. Joel is brilliantly creative and has been known to think well outside the box. In the case of Atlanta's marketing plans, he had even outdone himself.

As the city began to look at ways to take advantage of the worldwide exposure sure to come from hosting the 1996 Olympic Games, Joel had announced to the world that he intended to sell sponsorships to the city's parks and buildings, streets, and even street signs. With tongue firmly in cheek (I think), he was promoting laser beam ads to be bounced off the moon and, if that wasn't enough, he proposed to round up all the stray dogs in town and have advertising messages displayed on them. The national media had a field day with his pronouncements. Babbitt got a lot of ink for the city—and for himself—and the media had confirmed their early suspicions that we were as dumb and unsophisticated as they thought us to be.

I happened to be vacationing in the Virgin Islands when the *New York Times* ran the story on the city's marketing strategies. I was proudly wearing an Atlanta 1996 shirt to let everyone know that I was a part of this important history-making endeavor. When people in our hotel began to guffaw at the story, I quietly put my shirt away and began asking myself what I had gotten into. It wasn't the last time I was to ask that question.

Our meeting with the mayor was cordial, but tense. We wanted to be sure that they understood the restrictions as to what they could or could not do regarding the marketing of the Olympic Games. City Hall's feeling was that these were Atlanta's games, not just the committee's. The sparring continued through the meeting until one of the mayor's chief aides had had enough. He slammed his hand down on the table and exclaimed, "What good is it to have the Olympic Games in Atlanta if we can't make a buck off them." That view was to prevail through the end of the Games three and a half years later. Bill Campbell succeeded Maynard Jackson as mayor of Atlanta in 1994, but the "make a buck" philosophy remained intact and it caused the city to look like a third-rate flop house when the world came to see us in July 1996.

There is more than enough blame to go around. There are the small-minded folks in city government, a timid business community fearful of being labeled racist, a local media that has little, if any, influence in how things work in town, and our own belief that the Olympic Games were so positive that somehow its goodness would override the problems inherent in the city.

To know all you need to know about Atlanta, walk around the city today (but not after dark) and look. It is almost as if the Centennial Olympic Games were never here. The hope and promise and expectation that greeted Billy Payne in his triumphant return to Atlanta are dim memories. There are some signs to be sure—the new baseball stadium, Centennial Olympic Park, dormitories for Georgia State University overlooking our downtown freeway system, and new football stadiums at Morris Brown College and Clark Atlanta—all gifts of the Atlanta Committee for the Olympic Games. Some public housing projects have been torn down and rebuilt as mixed-income development. But the belief that having the Games in Atlanta would solve all our social and economic problems was naïve. It didn't even put us up there with the great cities of the world. In fact, if the Games did anything, they exposed our weaknesses—a preoccupation with race and a lack of leadership—that we seem unable to admit to ourselves, let alone anybody else.

It is important here that "Atlanta" be defined. According to the Metro Area Chamber of Commerce, the Atlanta Metropolitan area covers some twenty counties with some 3.6 million people (almost half the population of the state of Georgia) and a per capita income of over $31,000. The area grew by 660,000 people from the time the Olympics were awarded to Atlanta until today. The U.S. Bureau of Labor Statistics ranks it the eleventh largest metropolitan area in the country. Most of the people in this "Atlanta" have either moved out of the city or came here from somewhere else and settled. The result has been a number of formerly rural towns that now are sophisticated urban centers.

A perimeter highway rings the city and has been responsible for moving businesses closer to where people live. That, in turn, has brought huge shopping complexes, theatres, restaurants, and other amenities to affluent suburbanites who rarely travel downtown anymore. One of the comments I heard most from friends who enjoyed the Games was how long it had been since they had been downtown.

Interestingly, the region has no boundaries. There are no bodies of water, mountain chains or nearby cities to keep people from moving further and further away. And they do. As suburban areas grow crowded with people, fast food chains, and clogged highways, folks pick up and move further out (mostly north) and then repeat the process a few years later.

The city of Atlanta, however, is a totally different matter. It contains just over 425,000 people is 70% black and poor and only last year broke the cycle of losing population. The gains were modest and I attribute that as much to people worn out from two-hour commutes as I do to any quality of life improvement the city can offer.

In my role as a newspaper columnist, I hear from people who have moved back into the city and persevere in spite of an environment that is less than user-friendly. They describe the frustration of having no place to shop (only Macy's department store remains downtown), no grocery stores, dry cleaners, hardware stores, and so on, but they do find an abundance of street corner panhandlers and homeless people and an indifferent city bureaucracy. They frequently refer to themselves as "urban pioneers."

You would never know there is anything wrong with the city, however, if you listened to our sloganeering. We claim that we are "The Next Great International City" and "A City too Busy to Hate," neither of which are true but that doesn't stop us from bragging. It is a fundamental part of our culture. A favorite jibe at Atlanta by outsiders is that, "If the town could suck like it can blow, the Atlantic Ocean would be at its doorstep."

After joining the committee and traveling overseas frequently, I was amazed to find out what the volunteers had already learned in their quest for the Games: many Europeans had no idea where "The Next Great International City" was. One of the stories of the bid effort is the IOC member who reportedly told Billy Payne of his preference to have Atlanta host the 1996 Games. It was one of the first expressions of support that the bid committee had received. While the member extolled the many virtues of Atlanta, he mainly enjoyed the gambling establishments in the city. The only problem is that Atlanta has no gambling establishments. It turns out he was talking about Atlantic City. That story may have been embellished over time, but it proves a point that we aren't nearly as well known as we think we are.

We also aren't too busy to hate. The powerful element of racism still permeates the city. When the conservative Southeastern Legal Foundation filed suit against the City of Atlanta's minority vendor program in 1999, the reaction from black city and state officials was swift and ugly. Black political leaders encouraged people to picket the homes of Foundation board members (which is illegal) and block them as they tried to go to their "debutante balls." The Foundation was compared to the Ku Klux Klan. One state legislator said, "I now have somebody to hate and I hate Matt Glavin [the Foundation's president.]" Neither Glavin nor the Southeastern Legal Foundation had done anything illegal. They had challenged the city's race-based affirmative action program. (Interestingly, no race-based program like the city's has been approved in the courts since 1989.) For that, Glavin's life and that of his family were threatened and he had to have police protection. He was run off the road twice. He found his tires flattened from nails. His sin was in not backing off when political leaders yelled "race" at the top of their lungs.

The lawsuit is a sad example of what is wrong with Atlanta. Nobody can compromise. While Mayor Bill Campbell was declaring in the press a "fight to the death" in defense of city's set-aside program, and promising that "we will not be browbeaten into submission by any judge," the Metro Atlanta Chamber of Commerce was announcing plans to spend $200,000 for ads confirming their support of "equal opportunity." They should have been attempting to get all parties together, work out an amenable solution, and tone down the rhetoric, but found themselves powerless to influence the mayor in the city "Too Busy to Hate."

Flying back to Atlanta with members of the governor's staff and the mayor's office from a White House meeting, I asked Campbell's aide who in the business community the mayor listened to. "Nobody," he said. I was surprised. "Why not?" "Because," he replied as though talking to a freshman political science student, "business doesn't deliver votes." I found that enlightening—and sad.

The Atlanta I grew up in had a reputation as a can-do city with a strong business-political connection. Even in the days of segregation, the city was a liberal light in an otherwise unprogressive region of the country. There was an unusually good dialogue between black and white leaders. One reason was the colleges of the historically black Atlanta University had turned out a large number of graduates who had stayed in Atlanta and had built a strong black middle class. Another reason was the enlightened leadership of William B. Hartsfield, who served as mayor of the city from 1938 to 1961.

The business leadership in Atlanta was in the banks, utilities, department stores, and the newspaper. A half dozen people could decide on a course of action for the city and ensure that it got done. Fortunately, the leadership was ethical and honest and had the best interests of the city in mind. In the early 1960s, the city of Atlanta was booming. That all changed with the civil rights struggle led by a native Atlantan, Dr. Martin Luther King, Jr. The good ol' boys network was gone and along with it, the harmful policy of "separate but equal." Blacks rightfully began to lay claim to their share of the economic pie. Atlanta's first black mayor was Maynard Jackson who was originally elected in 1974 and served until 1982. He came back in in 1990 for another four-year term. In assuming the office as mayor, Jackson decided to "level the field" and for the first time in history, whites had to share power. He began hiring more minorities and threatened to put an affirmative action program into the works for all businesses located in Atlanta. It was at that point that Atlanta didn't look quite as progressive as it once had. Whites began to cut and run from the city to the suburbs. Downtown businesses followed. Department stores were close behind. As time passed, the Atlanta banks began to be consolidated into out-of-state banks and headquarters moved. Most large companies in town like BellSouth and others were finding themselves increasingly in the international marketplace and, by necessity, were less focused on Atlanta. All of these dynamics created a racial divide between the political forces and the business community that has deepened and widened over the years.

In the meantime, the larger Atlanta was developing a strong infrastructure of superhighways and communications and a world-class airport operated by the city but to the benefit of the suburbanites. The climate was good; labor was plentiful, cheap and mostly non-union and there was plenty of real estate available. As the rest of the region was growing bigger and richer, the city was becoming poorer and blacker.

Through all the turbulent times, one thing did remain unchanged from the halcyon days of the early '60s: Atlanta's rah-rah attitude. It had just been moved beyond the city limits. I am positive that no other city could have created a Billy Payne. No other city could have considered an idea as wild as his possible. We just didn't know better. Granted, it helped to have another dreamer in City Hall in the person of Andrew Young to give it sanction, but in Atlanta, having a group of volunteers win the bid to host the Olympic Games on their first try seemed totally logical. That is the endearing side of the city.

When the city won the bid, which I liken to the dog that caught the car, reality set in large doses. Starting with the fight between Jackson and Payne over who was going to be in control of the planning—and money—through the city's ambush marketing program and even to the last day when one of our employees caught the city's marketing contractor putting up unauthorized banners along the marathon route—the IOC charter allows no advertising in any Olympic venue, including the marathon—and got himself arrested, it was less a collaborative effort with the city and more of a competitive battle.

I will have more to say about them in the chapter on the media, but suffice it to say that the *Atlanta Journal-Constitution*, along with most of the media in town, did not do as good of a job as they could have in placing expectations on the city to be ready for the world's spotlight. Not unlike the politicians, the media saw dollar signs from the advertising they would sell by having the Olympic Games in Atlanta.

Once the conscience of the city, the newspaper has lost influence as Atlanta has lost population. The mayor and his constituents—mostly inner city blacks—routinely ignore them. The whites that live in the northern arc of the Atlanta area tend to be more conservative and view the Atlanta newspapers as liberal and therefore biased.

Consequently, the paper had little leverage to insist that the city get its act together for the Games. We expected the attention and it was deserved. After all, this was the largest thing to ever happen in Atlanta and people had a right to know we were doing what we said we were going to do. But the same zeal was not applied to the efforts "outside the fence." Had it been, I am convinced the rest of the world would have seen a much better city than it did. In my opinion, the media must share some of the blame for the city's performance during the Games—something the media are not very good at doing.

There were two high profile issues that dominated our relationship with the city. One was the city services contract, and the other was the city's ambush marketing efforts.

While the Games were spread over the state, the majority of the venues would be located in the city limits of Atlanta. Billy Payne had already won the battle over who was going to control the $500 million in construction contracts and it wasn't going to be City Hall. Even though final approval would be through the Metropolitan Atlanta Olympic Games Authority and the mayor sat on that body, Atlanta had lost a lot of financial leverage in that decision. So the next best thing was to charge us for everything they thought they could get away with—starting with a business license. While we were legally a not-for-profit corporation by law, the Atlanta City Council in their wisdom, deemed that we should pay a business license like any business coming into town.

I didn't have a lot of direct contact with the city over these issues. That privilege belonged to Shirley Franklin, who had a long career in city hall politics, A. D. Frazier, because of the large amount of dollars at play in the negotiations, Richard Stogner, former chief administrative officer to Maynard Jackson, and Pat Glisson, ACOG chief of finance, who had performed that role in city government. It was an excellent team, wise in the ways of city politics, including all the race cards that Atlanta was always prepared to play.

My interest in the city was twofold. I had responsibility for state and federal relations. The three levels of government were intertwined operationally and politically. The president was up for reelection just three months after the Centennial Games. Governor Miller was one of his most ardent supporters and the City of Atlanta was a Democratic stronghold. While that made our job somewhat easier because of the commonality of interests, dealing with them on a one-on-one basis could be very difficult. Each unit of government had their own demands of us and should we fail to meet them, they could pick up the phone and complain. It wasn't so much the city calling the state, as it was the city and state calling the White House. Sometimes, when they couldn't agree, they just put us in the middle.

In the 1995 session of the General Assembly, the lawmakers put forth legislation that would place all Olympic security matters under the Georgia Department of Public Safety. The state legislature has long considered Atlanta's government incompetent of operating anything more complex than a two-car funeral. They certainly didn't want them responsible for planning security for the Games. The city's reaction was predictable: The bill was racist; we were somehow responsible (actually, we opposed it); they would stop negotiating on the city services agreement and send out an announcement requesting that other nations not participate in the Games. I had a hard time understanding why Finland or Fiji gave a tinker's damn whether the state coordinated security planning or not, but evidently the city government knew something I didn't.

My other interest was the image that the city was projecting around the world. One of the responsibilities of someone in my job is to remind people that we tend to see the world "inside out," meaning that we think our internal priorities match the priorities of the public. We need to remember the "outside in" view. That is the more important perspective. That is what the public thinks of us. It is not often that those two views coincide. For example, while the city of Atlanta and ACOG had staked out the operational and financial issues between them, the public didn't know the difference. The further away you got, the more the issues were about "Atlanta." To the public, it was Atlanta that seemed to be having problems, not the city government or the organizing committee. As the decibel levels got louder and the issues more complex, the perception only increased. Could Atlanta be ready in time for the Olympic Games?

But when you are locked in hand-to-hand combat over dollars and power, that doesn't seem important to the combatants. It is strictly "inside out" thinking. That attitude would come back to haunt all of us at Games time.

In January 1996, after an up and down year of negotiating, ACOG and the city finally had a city services agreement in which we would compensate the city for services rendered above those that were considered normal for such things as police and fire services, garbage collection, and street closings during the Games. The city service contract was a part of the TriParty Agreement between the city, the Metropolitan Atlanta Olympic Games Authority, and ACOG and was vague in how the parties would arrive at what were "normal" services and what were "extraordinary." The city had started negotiations by asking for everything remotely connected with the Olympic Games. Even though the city would be richer by over $200 million from the construction of Olympic venues and in additional tax revenues, we looked like a fat financial target. A bond referendum passed in 1994 for infrastructure repairs was being referred to as the "Olympic Bond Issue," meaning that if the budget didn't allow sufficient dollars for servicing the debt, taxes would have to be raised and ACOG would be a convenient scapegoat for causing the tax increase. At one point, the city proposed that we give them $10 million. It would be like a draw. Every time they spent some money on our behalf, they would draw down on the pool of funds. When that money was depleted we would replenish. It was like giving them an unlimited expense account. That was totally unacceptable. Their attitude was to ignore all the money that the Olympic Games would bring to Atlanta and, instead, consider us nothing more than a "cost causer." Only in Atlanta.

By the time negotiations were finished, city services would cost us $9.5 million in cash, plus another $1.5 million of in goods and services we would provide them and $4 million that my department had gotten from the Department of Justice to help offset police overtime. We thought it was a good deal. The city council approved but with an amendment instructing the mayor to come back and negotiate for more money. Ominously, the agreement also codified the terms for the city's own marketing program.

This responsibility fell to Munson Steed, a political ally of Mayor Bill Campbell whom the mayor handpicked for the job. He was hired to lease public property, sell souvenirs, and manage street vending during the Games. Nothing was said about bouncing laser beams off the moon and little billboards on stray dogs, for which we could be thankful, but after the street vendors program was finished, Joel Babbitt's ideas were looking better and better.

Steed announced plans to raise $50 million for the city. He would sell sponsorships to whoever paid him top dollar, Olympic sponsor or not.

The International Olympic Committee had a point about the city's marketing program. In their way of thinking, Atlanta was indemnified from any costs of putting on the 1996 Games. The city was getting worldwide exposure and hundreds of millions of dollars of facilities. In fact, the IOC was not particularly happy with Billy's idea of building for afterlife and retrofitting for the Games. That was especially true of the main stadium that was, in fact, a baseball stadium. It was here that the opening and closing ceremonies and the track and field events were to be held and it was being modified to accommodate these high profile events. (The late Primo Nebiolo, the imperious head of International Amateur Athletic Federation that governed track and field, was furious over the decision to have his athletes compete in a "baseball stadium.")

While we still needed to raise a lot of money from sponsors to cover the costs of privately-funded Games, we now found ourselves in open competition with the City of Atlanta, who was conducting a highly visible ambush-marketing program. Michael Payne, the IOC's marketing director, said in a newspaper interview that never in history had a city that "has not one penny in the organizing of the Olympic Games" tried to turn around and compete with the organizing committee.

Our friends in the Olympic movement were having a hard time understanding the logic of all of this, and so was I. But we weren't the only ones. We had some good company. George Fischer, chief executive officer of Kodak, was apoplectic over the city's plans to make a deal with Fuji, his largest competitor. Kodak was a worldwide sponsor of the Games and carried a lot of clout with the IOC. Fisher was threatening to pull his company out of the Games.

Dick Pound, the Canadian lawyer who chaired the IOC's coordination commission and was the overseer of the organization's marketing efforts, ripped the city for their misguided efforts and received a non-contrite reply in return. Sometimes the light bulb is slow to go off in my head, but it was this incident that finally brought me to the firm conclusion that the city really didn't care how they looked, how they acted, or whether the Olympic Games fared well. They were going to make as much money off the event as possible. The "make a buck" philosophy reigned. It was compounded by business leaders afraid to tell the mayor what a spectacle he was creating lest they be smeared as racists, a local newspaper convinced that the world's image of Atlanta was inextricably tied to Izzy, the blue slug of a mascot that the paper loved to hate, and not to the Munson Steed vendors program.

The mayor's plan originally called for a controlled vending program that would give 170 vendors exclusive right to sell certain products for a cool $10,000 fee. However, the city's attorneys decided that was illegal, and that the vending program—which was under a lot of heat from the politically connected Black Vendors Association—should be open to all. That meant that for $150 anybody could set up shop on the streets of Atlanta. Over 6,000 did.

The result was chaotic. Vendors lost money. Some lost their life savings. Downtown looked like a small town carnival on steroids. Tacky is too nice a word to describe the city during the Games.

As if the thousands of hawkers and the ramshackle huts weren't bad enough, the vendors choked the sidewalks, making access very difficult. Every day during the Games we met at 8:00 AM with the IOC board and they would critique our previous day's performance and point out areas for improvement. Every day they complained about the traffic tie-ups around their headquarters at the Marriott Marquis. Every day, Bill Rathburn would be charged with calling the Atlanta police to have them do a better job of directing traffic. Every day on my two-block walk back to Inforum—our headquarters—following that meeting, I would see the police—usually five or six—sitting under an umbrella, reading the paper and ignoring the traffic jam that stretched for several blocks. It was maddening.

The police were angry with the mayor over pay issues and they expressed their disapproval by making us all look bad. There was one shining exception. Major John Woodward, who was our liaison, did his best to keep things working, but he was fighting an uphill battle from the start. He deserved better.

The one branch of city government that worked as it should was the Department of Aviation, specifically the airport. We had to get a lot of people into the country, processed, and on their way as quickly as possible. We also had to get them back out of town just as efficiently and just as quickly. Angela Giddens and her colleague James Stogner were the airport general managers and tough people to deal with. They were as demanding of us as we were of them, but unlike most of the people in the Atlanta city government, you could rely on their word. As a result, the airport operation was near flawless. Shortly after the Games the mayor fired Giddens. Beyond this group and Norm Copeland, Director of the Bureau of Buildings, help was scant at City Hall.

Meanwhile back downtown, once the Games were concluded, the inevitable lawsuits followed the vending debacle. While some vendors got some remuneration; most did not. Munson Steed was sued for $25 million. The suit was thrown out of court. Nobody made these unfortunate souls sign up for his program.

Even today, Bill Campbell is totally unrepentant about the way Atlanta performed during the Games and why not? The city netted $2.5 million and Steed made almost $2 million. But Atlanta had paid dearly for its reputation.

Today, the city is back to business as usual. There are new facilities, but the old attitudes are still there. Bill Campbell is finishing up his second term as mayor. The Atlanta newspapers editorialized against his reelection in 1997, having discovered in blinding hindsight that he "gratuitously insults business leaders and suburban politicians who are in a position to help the city. He refuses to acknowledge that Atlanta has become a small and rather powerless community in a sprawling, prosperous region. Even now, after the debacle of the vending program led by Munson Steed's B. G. Swing Games Management, Inc., Campbell defends it. It is helpful to remember that he turned away opponents of the program with the charge that their criticism was racist." I never asked but I am curious when the paper had first made this startling discovery. Incidentally, their rebuke didn't make any difference. The mayor won reelection with 53% of the vote in a runoff. Only 29% of the eligible voters participated in the election.

Bill Campbell will leave office with no legacy other than he happened to be in office when the Centennial Olympic Games came to Atlanta. Nothing more.

The people of Atlanta, however, seem to have had a great time while the Games were here. Even these many years after the Games, people still say "thank you" for the effort and recount some favorite story. They will have their great memories forever.

As for me, I will always be disappointed that Atlanta didn't give Billy Payne the tickertape parade after the Games that they did before. The city can never repay him for what he did. He has quietly gone on with his life, but for one magic moment, he presented the city to the world. It should have been our finest hour, but we—city government, the business community, the media, ACOG—found out that saying you are a world class city is one thing; being one is totally different.

You've seen these chairs many times. It is where the president entertains important dignitaries in the Oval Office. On this night, they were occupied by Billy and Martha Payne before the torch arrived at the White House. (*author's collection*)

ACOG CEO Billy Payne and Chief Operating Officer A. D. Frazier compare notes before a meeting with the IOC executive board at Chateau de Vidy in Lausanne. (*author's collection*)

Billy and Don Mischer, who produced the Opening and Closing
Ceremonies confer with IOC vice president, Dick Pound, a Canadian
and chairman of the Atlanta coordination commission. Ginger
Watkins looks on. (*author's collection*)

Don Mischer and I celebrate a good meeting with the IOC in front of
the Chateau de Vidy with Charlie Battle, managing director—international relations and one of the original volunteers. Charlie was one
of the best liked and most respected individuals in the Olympic
movement. (*author's collection*)

One of my most memorable moments was seeing the field where the ancient Olympic Games had been held 27 centuries earlier. Spectators sat on the banks. It was here where the flame was lit that arrived in Atlanta 100 days later. (*author's collection*)

Georgia Governor Zell Miller was in Los Angeles to greet the Atlanta contingent. He had been one of our sternest critics but became a great supporter. He's drinking ice water! (*author's collection*)

The torch was passed at Central High School in Little Rock, Arkansas, in one of the many dramatic moments along the 16,000 mile route. At far right, Mack McLarty, our liason at the White House and a great friend, along with Little Rock Mayor Jim Daily. (*author's collection*)

Ann Holder, wife of ACOG cochairman Bob Holder, and Jane enjoy the day for IOC spouses at the White House. Little did they know of the negotiating it took to get them there. (*author's collection*)

Running the torch in Cartersville, Georgia—my mother's birthplace—escorted by my son, Ken, left, and son-in-law, Ted Wansley. It was an unforgettable experience for me and the boys. (*photo by Maribeth Wansley*)

Awaiting us at the end were Jane and my most important audience, grandsons (L-R) Thomas Yarbrough, Nicholas Wansley, Brian Yarbrough, and Zack Wansley. They ended up seeing more Olympic events than their granddad. (*photo by Maribeth Wansley*)

The U.S. Olympic team enters the packed stadium in Atlanta. It was the night we—and the world—had been waiting for. (*photo by Maribeth Wansley*)

The family was able to enjoy the festivities together, a real treat for me. (L-R) With me are Jackie Yarbrough, son Ken, Jane, Ted Wansley, daughter Maribeth. (*author's collection*)

Hillary Clinton at the Winter Olympics in Lillehammer, Norway. I introduced myself to her and said, "Since we are away from home on Valentine's Day, let's get our picture made together." She said, "Let's do," and handed the camera to a Secret Service Agent. (*author's collection*)

An outpouring of grief at the site of the Centennial Olympic Park bombing. If the intent of the bombing was to intimidate, it was a failure. In fact, it brought people closer together. (*photo by Maribeth Wansley*)

To celebrate the Centennial anniversary of the modern Olympics, the Hellenic Olympic Committee invited us to a gala in Athens. We were greeted by mayor Dimitris Avramopolous. L to R, I am with Billy Payne, Ginger Watkins, Charlie Battle, and Mayor Avramopolous. (*author's collection*)

L to R, Charlie Battle, Ginger Watkins, Billy Payne, A. D. Frazier, Don Mischer, Dick Yarbrough, Dave Maggard, and Bob Brennan at the IOC headquarters. (*author's collection*)

President Clinton passes the torch to Carla McGhee, a member of the U.S. gold medal basketball team. A few years earlier, she had been injured in an automobile accident and some thought she might never walk again. Note the Georgia State Trooper just in front of the flags. The state patrol escorted the flame across the nation and did us proud. (*courtesy of the White House*)

Sanford Stadium at the University of Georgia, hosting the women's Olympic soccer finals. It was the largest crowd to ever view a women's sporting event. The U.S. team won the gold medal. (*courtesy of the University of Georgia/photo by Rick O'Quinn*)

Jane and I anxiously await the arrival of the Olympic Flame in Los Angeles. I didn't see much of her for the three-and-a-half years I was at ACOG and this was a good chance for her to share in the excitement. (*author's collection*)

# 9

## MANAGING THE UNMANAGEABLE

*The press technology is not working and they are taking it out on us.*
— Diary Entry, July 21, 1996

I find it ironic that the public relations business has a suspect image. After all, we are in the image business, aren't we? Unfortunately, doing your job correctly means you will likely have either your organization or the media mad at you—sometimes both. That isn't the way to foster a good image.

I speak from experience. Until I retired and decided to cross over and join them, I have been called every name imaginable by the media. At various times, I have been referred to as "flack," "whore," "Svengali," "control freak," and worse. My favorite was "worthless," a sobriquet laid on me by Atlanta columnist Colin Campbell. In his case, I remembered what my daddy said—consider the source. You attract the criticism because you have something the media wants: information. Information is the oxygen that keeps them alive. If you don't give them what they want when they want it, they will do whatever they can to get it, including beating up on you. It's not personal, although I could never convince my wife of that. It's just the nature of the business.

Meanwhile, inside the company, if you are doing your job correctly, you are suspect to your management. Managers fall into two general categories regarding the media: They either underestimate the power of the press—and broadcasters—thinking they can charm their way through any media contact or, if not, ignore them altogether. The other group—and by far the most prevalent—are convinced that reporters stay awake at night thinking of how they can screw them and the company. It is a conspiracy theory as old as the Gutenberg press. Therefore the poor PR person is put in the position of reminding management that the media is *not* the audience. They are merely the "pass through" to the many publics who have a stake in how you do business. In order to get to those publics with correct information, you have to deal with the media. They are the gatekeepers. Yet, that argument tends to make you look as if you are a part of the conspiracy. Sometimes I feel like if I had gotten a dollar for every time I heard, "Whose side are you on, anyway?" I could have retired a wealthy man at a very young age.

The public relations person is caught squarely in the middle. Thus, many PR people just decide to go with the flow. They will do whatever their management tells them to do and they will work overtime to be loved by the media.

I started out in broadcasting and somehow got into public relations at Southern Bell some years later. My education in the business was on-the-job training. I had a great mentor, Jasper Dorsey, who taught me that I could be liked or I could be effective but I couldn't be both. I decided to be effective. While I never won any popularity polls at BellSouth or at ACOG, I took the position that what I did was as important as what the attorneys did.

So to make sure the external environment got represented in management decisions, I could get adversarial and I will say that I won my share of arguments on how to deal with the external environment, including the media. Having a CEO that will listen to you helps and fortunately both John Clendenin and Billy Payne listened and accepted much of what I counseled, although Mr. Clendenin once suggested that I not look at him like "You dumb s---," when he did turn me down.

On the media side, I had a reputation as someone who was significant in the business. Like dogs smell fear, the media can detect those who can speak for a company and those who can't. I had earned an enviable reputation for being able to tell a reporter that a rumor wasn't true and have them take my word for it. That kind of reputation comes only from being absolutely honest with the media. You never, ever lie even if the bad news is embarrassing to the organization. Over the long haul, it will pay dividends.

So, with a reputation as being effective in the business and respected by the media, I was a natural choice for Bob Holder, the co-chairman of the board to present me to Billy Payne for his consideration to become a part of the management team at the Atlanta Committee for the Olympic Games.

The media, particularly the *Atlanta Journal-Constitution* was glad to see me come. I was the first high-profile hire at the senior level since A. D. Frazier had joined a few years earlier. My arrival was accompanied by a large story by reporter Melissa Turner with the headline, "A Flaming Torch for Summer Games." I'm still not sure what that meant, but the story was very positive. After the Games, she pretty much held me responsible for most of the glitches, calling me "arrogant."

The Atlanta paper had been involved from the beginning as Billy Payne and his small band of volunteers had traveled around the world in their quixotic mission. They witnessed and reported on the comings and goings of the IOC members to Atlanta. There were no secrets. The bid effort, after all, was a long shot at best. That is why I find it amusing to witness the newspaper's righteous indignation that occurred after the Games when they demanded that ACOG open all its records. I doubt there is anything in the boxes that they didn't already know. They were there when it occurred.

My first impression upon joining ACOG and meeting the reporters assigned to the coverage of the organization was that someone had given a bunch of ten year olds keys to a new Porsche—no one knew how to drive but nobody else had one. I was told almost upon arrival by Bert Roughton, one of the reporters who had been assigned the ACOG beat from the beginning that, "We (his paper) will dictate the coverage of the media worldwide." Somehow, I couldn't see the *New York Times*, the *Wall Street Journal, USA TODAY, Le Monde, Financial Times*, etc., being influenced by what came out of the *Atlanta Journal-Constitution*.

Probably my biggest frustration during my tenure at the Atlanta Committee was defending the Atlanta papers to the national media, who didn't consider them near the peer that the locals thought themselves to be.

That was not always the case. I had grown up reading the editorials of Ralph McGill, editor of the *Atlanta Constitution* from 1942 to 1960. A Pulitzer Prize winner, McGill was an impassioned crusader for equal rights and was known as the "Conscience of the South." He was passionate in his cause and the paradigm of what all good journalists should be. His editorials were widely denounced by segregationists, and politicians around the state vilified him but he would not be intimidated from stating his views. You may not have liked Ralph McGill but you had to respect him and the management of the paper for backing his unpopular views.

The greatness had left the paper with McGill and his successor, Gene Patterson, long ago and the Olympic Games looked like a sure way of getting back in the big leagues.

My honeymoon was quickly over. One of the conditions I had made with Billy was that all media requests would come through me (which earned me the title of "control freak"). In turn, I would guarantee that the person they were requesting to talk to would be available. That was good news and bad news for the papers. Since their chummy relationship with Billy had begun during the early days of the bid period, reporters were used to calling up whomever they wanted and getting whatever they needed. The organization was too big and too complex for that now. At the same time, there were managers in the organization that wouldn't talk to the media, given their own choice. This way, I could know who was talking to whom and stop some of the incessant leaks coming out of ACOG and yet assure reporters of getting to the subject matter experts they needed. This was the way I had worked at BellSouth and the arrangement had been satisfactory all the way around. But the reaction at the paper was immediate and indignant. I was told by reporters that the paper would continue to call anybody they chose. Fine, I said. Only they aren't going to talk to you. I was tested and fortunately the word was out around the building to get the requests back to me. The employees did just that and we were able to settle into an uneasy truce over that issue that lasted through the Games.

However, I almost wasn't around to see it. I came close to losing my job a few months later. It was one of those situations I described earlier about getting caught in the middle—a bad place to be. In the early days of the organizing committee before I arrived, a deal had been made between ACOG and the media on open records. In essence, we said we would share everything but marketing information and financial records. Under the law as a non-profit, we could limit what we chose for release, but that would be bad policy, given the ancillary impact our efforts would have on governmental agencies. So a deal was brokered. One of the things we agreed to was the salary information of the five highest paid employees. From the time of the agreement, however, the management structure had changed. Instead of executive vice presidents and senior vice presidents, our titles, except for Payne and Frazier, were changed to managing director in early 1993. However, the changes in title and in what we reported publicly would have to be approved by the board of directors. Coming out of a corporate background, that made inordinate sense to me. Certainly, BellSouth would never undertake such actions without approval from its board.

Before the board meeting, the paper wanted to see salaries for the fifteen managing directors. Not until the board approves. However, I said, I will give you the five top salaries and after board approval, the rest. To say the newspaper overreacted is an understatement. Headlines screamed "ACOG Retreats From Promises of Openness." The attorney general, running hard as a stealth candidate for governor, sided with the paper and said "state and local governments — and not ACOG — are ultimately responsible for staging the Olympics." It made me wonder if he had read the Triparty agreement. The editorial cartoonist weighed in with a giant Izzy shaking a bewildered individual representing the public and saying, "It's None of Your @*.#<*.$. Business What I'm Up To." I figured the whole crowd was breathing into paper sacks to keep from hyperventilating. In retrospect, I think they were as incensed at being told no as they were at having to wait two months until the board approved.

I talked to the Olympics editor, Thomas Oliver, whom I had known for years and told him that the histrionics weren't going to get the material released any earlier and the more they protested, the more the organization would resist. Please work with me, I asked, and I will get it handled. To his credit, he chained his pit bulls and let me go to work inside.

There was no problem inside with giving the paper the information they wanted, just as soon as the board approved. Billy was in agreement and Horace Sibley, who provided our legal counsel, also agreed. Next, I went to my co-chairman, Bob Holder, and he, too, had no concerns about our releasing the salaries. It was going too easily .

I put together all the materials for the board meeting and went with Holder to the compensation committee of the board for their approval. Know this about boards of directors. The work of the board is done by committee. When a board convenes, committees make reports, discussion ensues and the actions are usually approved. So when the compensation committee gave its okay, we were home free. Or so I thought. I called Thomas Oliver at the paper and told him things had gone very smoothly. Billy Payne had approved the proposal, Holder had okayed it, and the compensation committee had no problem with it. It just needed a perfunctory blessing by the board and I would have the salary information in time for the morning paper.

That was a mistake. When the issue got before the board, I was sitting in the back of the room feeling pretty proud of myself. I had managed the situation perfectly. I had been influential in one of my first management recommendations inside the business and I had shown the newspaper that I had clout. Then to my shock, the board erupted. No way we were going to give the *Atlanta Journal-Constitution* anything more than the absolute minimum. Once we give them salaries then they are going to want more and more—the "camel's nose under the tent" argument. Finally, Andrew Young called for quiet and I thought that maybe, just maybe, he could turn the issue around. After all, he had a worldwide reputation as a peacemaker. Another mistake. Young adamantly opposed giving them the information. "Let them sue," he said. I was stunned. I had put myself into an untenable position. I had been overruled by the board and had shown the *Atlanta Journal Constitution* that I didn't have the influence they presumed I did. I would have to resign. In fact, I leaned over to my friend, Bill Moss and said, "Looks like I'm gone." Eight months on the job and my Olympic career shot.

At that point, two gentlemen who deserve recognition, Bill Ides, former president of the American Bar Association, and Hugh Chapman, president of NationBank's Georgia operations, argued for disclosures. Bob Holder also took up the cause as well as Billy and Horace Sibley. The disclosure issue finally passed but no one seemed happy about it.

On shaky legs, I walked back to my office to call Oliver. I told him I had the information. "That's good," he said, "I'm dropping the law suit we were going to file in the trash can as we speak." We had dodged a bullet but I was taking no chances. "If the paper decides to do a 'what this black manager makes compared to this white manager' or 'how this female compares to this male', I will be a dead duck," I told him. "Don't make my job harder than it already is." He gave me his word and the coverage was excellent. I was given due credit for having had a role in the change—if the reporters only knew—and they published the salaries, a couple of sidebar stories and an editorial. As for the "camel's nose under the tent," we would continue to have fights with the paper over other issues, but not salaries. By 1996 we had to call them and remind them we had the salaries ready for them.

My biggest disappointment was that the editorial cartoonist, who had gotten so excited, didn't draw another picture of Izzy and the public holding hands and spooning in public. I thought about asking him, but I was afraid he would say, "@*.#<*.$."

I decided early that there were too many things going on at ACOG for two or three of us to handle. When I had arrived, my staff consisted of Donna Johnsson, on loan from Southern Company, and Bob Brennan, a long-time newsman, who had arrived at the Atlanta committee during the bid process from the Metropolitan Atlanta Rapid Transit Agency (MARTA). He was that agency's public information director. Prior to that time, he was news director at the CBS affiliate in Atlanta, WAGA. Bob had brought his hard-nosed, no-nonsense attitude to ACOG with him. He was officially the press chief, a title bestowed by the International Olympic Committee. This meant that he would have the authority for deciding who would receive that most precious of all commodities, the media credential. This allows the media access to the Games. Without it, you don't get in. Since there were more media by far who wanted to cover the Games than there were credentials to accommodate them, it was the one piece of leverage we had with the media. It was a leverage that we shared with the IOC and the USOC but it was our big hammer—a fact that Brennan delighted in reminding the media.

Besides Billy Payne, Bob Brennan was the one person who seemed most able to capture the goodness of the Olympic movement. I found that remarkable because his long years in the media business had given him the prerequisite crust of cynicism but not when it concerned the Olympics. This wasn't a job to him; it was a holy crusade.

But he hadn't helped the crusade by his impatience toward the media. That attitude, the missteps in the Augusta golf situation, and the political disputes over the stadium construction, had led to my coming to ACOG.

One of the first things I did was to identify and hire quality people and assign them to individual departments in ACOG. They would report to me but their assignment would be to assist the department for which they were responsible in whatever way the managing director of that department instructed. That way, we could be sure that our messages to the public—"On Time. On Target. On Schedule."—were consistent no matter what the situation. The individual units within the committee knew their own issues and would get the full attention of their appointed external counselor. It also gave us a fighting chance with the *Atlanta Journal-Constitution* who had reporters assigned to cover those individual departments.

The staff was excellent. I was amazed at the quality of the people attracted to the Olympic Games, when they were guaranteed that they would be out of a job in three years and would have accumulated no benefits in the meantime. Donna Johnsson became the department's deputy director. Simply stated, she supervised the staff on a day-to-day basis and kept up with the countless and mind-numbing details of the committee. This allowed me to give my attention to government relations and allowed me to focus much of my time in Washington where we were seeking security support, buses, manpower, materials, assurances of consistent immigration policies, etc.

Lyn May was responsible for the operations area and was our chief spokesperson. She also wrote Billy Payne's speeches. A former television anchor in Boston, Lyn had married a local *Atlanta Journal Constitution* columnist, Lee May, and moved to Atlanta. In all my years in the business, she is simply the most unflappable person I ever met. No matter how bad the situation, Lyn never panicked. She seemed to spend as much time assuring me that the sky hadn't fallen when I knew it had as she did patiently explaining to the media that, even if the sky did fall, our experts would have it back up tomorrow with all the stars in their original positions and sparkling. She did all of this with a smile.

I saw Lyn irritated just once and for good reason. John Huey, an Atlantan, who later became executive editor of *Fortune*, wrote a piece for the *New York Times* asserting that the Atlanta Games were nothing more than a rape and pillage of downtown Atlanta by a bunch of rich, white Republicans. He knew this since he was originally from Atlanta and, thus, wasn't compelled to talk to anybody at ACOG. His attack brought a harrumph from *Atlanta Journal Constitution* columnist Colin Campbell (I told you he harrumphed a lot) but since nobody seems to pay much attention to Campbell anyway, that didn't amount to much.

That is when sweet unflappable Lyn May stepped in. She wrote a terrific rebuttal saying how dare he try to speak for black people. (Huey is white; Lyn is African-American.) Among other things, she called him a pseudo-liberal (*zing*) and scored a direct hit. Huey called her and got the sweet smiling Lyn on the phone. She put the charm on him, arranged for him to go fishing with Billy Payne to find out what Payne was really like, instead of taking potshots. Huey ended up at *Fortune* doing a very positive piece on the people who only a short time earlier he had accused of rape and ruin. John Huey was no match for Lyn May.

Laurie Olsen came from a local public relations firm to handle games services, the Look of the Games, the ceremonies, among other things. Laurie was as pugnacious as Lyn May was unflappable. In fact, she more nearly fit the prototype of the people I usually hired. Since everybody feels in their heart that they are public relations experts, you need an "in-your-face" expert to remind them that they are not. Laurie Olsen could do that.

Scott Mall had dual responsibilities. He dealt with the public relations contacts at our sponsor and supplier companies but because of a strong government relations background, he assisted me in some of the complicated dealings we had with the federal government as well. He was also the hardest working of the group. I got to work at 6:00 AM every morning and one of the first things I did upon arriving was to start the coffee and then go speak to Scott. Sometimes, I think he spent the night at ACOG.

As the sponsorship program grew in ACOP, it became necessary for the marketing group to have a full-time person. Darby Coker, a former IBM'er and later owner of his own ad agency, was hired for that job and also worked in my organization. Keeping sponsors happy was no easy task.

One of the biggest elements of the Olympic Games was the Cultural Olympiad. In its own right, it was a huge enterprise that fell to Linda Stephenson, one of the original volunteers and was managed by Dr. Jeffrey Babcock. The Cultural Olympiad was of particular interest to the editor of the paper, Ron Martin. Because of the breadth of the endeavor—it would include everything from gathering all the Nobel Laureates in literature to art exhibits to country music—and the newspaper's strong interest in it, it needed someone who understood the arts as well as the media. For that job, I hired Susan Elliott, who had a strong background in arts. There would be others to come later and I wish I could name them all but space won't permit. We had attracted a great team.

Managing this or any other team would have been an impossibility without JoAnne Kessler, who came with me from BellSouth. To call her a secretary would be to grossly understate her work and influence. Before she started working for me at BellSouth, I had developed a reputation of being impossible to work for. One secretary, a veteran in the company, had told me she would quit before she would work for me another day. I was baffled. All I asked was that my secretary work ungodly hours, handle a million details, never make an error, and survive my temper tantrums. Against the advice of the other secretaries, Ms. Kessler decided to take the job. She was as low-key as I was high octane. She worked the hours, handled the details, never made a mistake, covered for me when I did, and became an indispensable part of my life. In fact, Jane, my wife, has said I was the only person in town with two wives — one at home, the other at work. Had JoAnne not come with me to the Atlanta Committee for the Olympic Games, I would not have survived the experience.

Even with a top-notch team in place, we still managed to shoot ourselves in the foot. Susan Elliott, assigned the Cultural Olympiad public relations responsibilities, is married to Rick Beard, head of the Atlanta History Center. He was also a member of the Cultural Olympiad advisory board. I hate surprises so imagine my shock to pick up the morning paper and read that Beard had written a letter, criticizing the lack of support for the work of his committee. To make sure we knew of his irritation, he sent copies to the members of his committee as well as to us and the complaint was shipped straight to the papers. This was big news because the suspicion lurked at the *Atlanta Journal-Constitution* that Billy Payne really wasn't that interested in the Cultural Olympiad and now they supposedly had proof. Proof from the husband of the wife assigned to handle the Cultural Olympiad. A wife who didn't know he was going to do this until he had done it. We managed to neutralize the story but not the suspicions. Those remained through the Games.

When it was in their interests, the media could be supportive. The Centennial Olympic Development Authority (CODA) was an outside agency charged with fixing up the city before the Olympics came to town. They had started with an agenda as ambitious as all the other groups trying to tap the presumed largesse the Games would bring. One of their efforts was to beautify Woodruff Park, which sits in the Five Points area of downtown. Once the hub of the city, Five Points was home to derelicts, drunks, panhandlers, pimps, and everything in between—not a particularly nice place to visit. Atlanta has a long history of advocacy for these groups. Sometimes I think the street people have more political power than the Chamber of Commerce.

When CODA broke ground for the park improvements, the homeless advocates disrupted the ceremony. After all, who wants a nice clean park in downtown Atlanta that might attract a nicer class of people? Because Woodruff Park is only a few blocks from the *Atlanta Journal Constitution* offices and because the *Atlanta Journal Constitution* offices are about all that remains in downtown, the protesters were savaged editorially. How dare the homeless people treat this event as they have done, the editors said. "To whom much is given, much is extorted." I thought that a wonderful line. As a matter of fact, I thought it applied to the whole town.

While the *Atlanta Journal-Constitution* had a large staff covering us intensely, we were also subject to coverage by the other local media. We didn't hear much from radio. They tend to report whatever they read in the paper. Four local stations covered us but most of their coverage was short, sound bite stuff. The TV stations didn't stay very close to the story. When a local politician demanded we pre-test all athletes for AIDS, we were besieged with calls about our policy on allowing athletes with AIDS to compete. That was not our decision. We simply provided the venues for the athletes to compete. The National Olympic Committees decided who would represent their country. In the United States, this was the USOC's decision. Everybody seemed to understand that but the medical reporter from WSB-TV. She called several members of our staff who referred her to the USOC. That didn't satisfy her. Even the staff who was used to talking to demanding reporters was taken aback at her rudeness. She wanted a talking head in Atlanta to explain our policy on AIDS. Period. I was in the car and she called me. I explained patiently (I thought) that we provide the venues, the countries decide who comes. As I was in the middle of my explanation, she hung up on me. I can't remember a reporter ever doing that.

Another television station dressed up a reporter as a homeless person and sent him to Centennial Park to see how he would be treated. That's okay except the reporter began to act in a bizarre manner and revealed a bulge under his shirt that could have been mistaken as a bomb. Undercover police stopped the undercover reporter and suggested he get the hell out of Dodge City and take his camera with him. Finally exhibiting some good sense, he left the park before getting himself in serious trouble. So much for show business.

Not surprisingly, the most comprehensive coverage came from WXIA, the NBC affiliate in town. They could be as tough on us as the others but they also knew they had a great prize on their hands and they spent more time understanding the issues before reporting them.

A thorn in the *Atlanta Journal Constitution's* side is the *Atlanta Business Chronicle*, a feisty weekly that covers the business news from every imaginable angle. They live for the opportunity to scoop their bigger rival but in doing so, could make a big story out of little stuff. For example, as the committee grew, we had to take additional quarters in another building nearby. Since Billy spent a good deal of his time in that building, too, it made sense to have an office there. That was a headline story in the *Business Chronicle*. I can't be too harsh on the *Chronicle*, however. I ended up writing a column for them for a couple of years. They are good people.

We were also getting some coverage in the early days from the national and the international press. Take this on faith from a native Southerner. There is a natural bias against the South in the national media and a natural bias against the U.S. in the rest of the world. If that sounds defensive or jingoistic, so be it. It's there. Our job was to convince the media from other parts that we had the talent and sophistication to put on good Olympic Games. That is why I have such anger at the city of Atlanta for their cheap flea market look. They met the world's low expectations.

The best publication by far was *USA TODAY*. They have a different culture from any newspaper with whom I have dealt over the years. Maybe it is because they pioneered a new kind of journalism. *USA TODAY* was the first to understand the impact of television and began presenting the news with shorter stories, more visuals and more color. Most papers that derided them ended up copying them because of their effectiveness. They were as hard on us as anybody, but their people, from the publisher, Tom Curley, down to the beat reporters, were classy people. Beyond copying their format, other media should copy their style as well.

The Atlanta Committee for the Olympic Games was neither as private as we wanted to be nor as public as the media demanded that we be. As I stated earlier, a deal had been worked out with the media on what information we would provide. It included, of course, salaries, executed contracts, financial plans (following submission to the ACOG Board of Directors and to MAOGA), and a host of other materials.

The Atlanta Newspapers are hard line on open records. While they consider seriously their mandate to serve the public, they don't like to be refused what they want, as was the case following the Games when they demanded to see what was in Billy Payne's private records.

One of the first tests after the salary incident occurred in early 1995 when the paper filed three Freedom of Information requests on us. They wanted all the information from the MAOGA auditors, Price Waterhouse, to get around the financial restrictions the paper had agreed to honor. Second, they wanted information on our earliest plans for the cycling and marathon courses. The City Council had that information but referred them to us. It is interesting to note that the City of Atlanta has an abominable record of honoring Freedom of Information requests. I wish the paper applied the same righteous indignation toward them that they did toward us. Maybe they are just inured to the fact that the city is going to ignore them, no matter what they do.

The third request was for our transportation plan, which was going to be hard to provide because in February 1995, we didn't yet have a transportation plan.

As for the cycling and marathon course, we told the City Council we would be happy to respond for them. We called the paper and told them we would be holding a media briefing on the status of the race courses and invited them to attend. They were stunned, but there was nothing they could do. They hadn't asked us for it; they had asked the city. So with great fanfare, we told them and all the other media about our plans at the same time.

The financial matter was a little more complicated. The paper had gone to MAOGA in order to check our finances. MAOGA didn't have the information. We said we had 60% of our money in the bank, 30% identified and were looking for the other 10%. We also had to have at least 5% of our uncommitted revenues in the bank to ensure that we had enough cash to cover some emergency that might occur. I couldn't understand the paper's timing. The time to have put us through this kind of questioning was two years ago. At this point, we were getting more confident of making our numbers than ever, although the 5% number was going to be close.

We were in constant negotiations with the paper over the financial issues and had been for weeks. A lawsuit would do them no good because by the time it was adjudicated, the Games would be over. We had reached no agreement by the next MAOGA meeting. At the meeting, the auditor, Robbie Pound, announced that we were at the 5% number. He casually mentioned that the number, which was about $34 million, was also about 2% of our total revenues. It was that last comment which the paper heard and the headlines that evening looked much as those on the day of Pearl Harbor must have looked. We had dropped from 5% to 2%. That didn't matter. The test wasn't total revenue. It was how much money we had in relation to uncommitted revenues. The editors immediately recognized the mistake and, to their credit, there was a balanced story by the next day.

Our fortunes with the paper ebbed and flowed. They would call and complain that every time they had a good investigative piece going, we would counter by holding a media briefing. I guess openness is in the eyes of the beholder.

As the Games grew closer, so did the national and international attention. Everybody came into town asking to interview Billy Payne. If he had chosen to do so, he could have spent every waking hour doing individual media interviews, so we had to pick and choose. For the most part, we held media briefings that would attract as many as 200 media personnel from all over the world.

The most notable of all the media briefings occurred when most of us were out of town. It was the day that Scott Mall earned his stripes. A. D. Frazier and I were flying to California to meet Billy Payne and the original band of volunteers who were bringing the torch to Los Angeles for the start of the relay across the United States. Also on the plane were Steve Wrigley, Governor Zell Miller's chief of staff, and Buddy Nix, the head of the Georgia Bureau of Investigation. About mid-flight they called us up to the front of the plane to tell us that as we spoke, the GBI, FBI, and Bureau of Alcohol, Tax and Firearms (ATF) were raiding and arresting members of a militia group in Middle Georgia. Agents had long ago infiltrated the assemblage and when the members began constructing incendiary devices, decided to move in and make arrests.

The reason for letting us know was the implications of Olympic terrorism. In this case, we were told, the plotters had a different target. They were mad at the government. We had our information from two sources about as reputable as they come. Better, in fact, than CBS which breathlessly began reporting that the bombers were planning to attack the Olympic Games according to their "sources," which, of course, they didn't have to identify. At the time of the announcement, Scott Mall was hosting a luncheon of some 200 members of the media that would be covering the Games. I have a picture in my files of Scott surrounded and besieged by several hundred microphones, cameras and reporters. Fortunately, he lived to fight another day.

We had the same situation awaiting us when we landed at Los Angeles. Fortunately, we also had Buddy Nix. He was able to calm and, perhaps, disappoint the gathered media by giving them the absolute facts. CBS stuck by their story. How they could still do so baffles me. My only explanation is that in today's hyper-competitive world, the inclination to be first with a story is so compelling that it sometimes gets in the way of good reporting. That kind of reporting wasn't the first I had seen and it sure won't be the last. If anything, the pressures on reporters to get the story out before the competition does is worsening. The rush to judgment on Richard Jewell case is a good example.

One of the things I didn't handle well was press operations. I should have left well enough alone. This department, which was in A. D. Frazier's operations, was responsible for the housing, feeding, transporting, and equipping of the media and for the press operations center, which was located in our headquarters at Inforum. The IOC makes no bones about it: the press is a major constituency. The members of the press expect preferred treatment and they get it. Unfortunately, it is never good enough to suit them. They are a notorious bunch of whiners. In our case, however, they had some justification. Just about everything that could go wrong did.

After a couple of years on the job, I insisted on having press operations report to me. I wasn't comfortable—with all due respects to A. D. and his team—that the press would get the kind of preferential treatment they and the IOC were expecting. After all, they were just another constituency to be housed, fed, and bused around to the venues. Putting them in my organization would ensure that the people who dealt with them on a day-to-day basis and would give them their credentials, would also be their advocates in the operations end of the Games. Bad decision. I had the responsibility and the advocacy. I just didn't have leverage. I also didn't have the right people in the job and went through three press operations managers until I finally turned the whole thing over to Donna Johnsson, my deputy.

The international press had been promised high-tech Games by IBM and by us. For those who signed up, we promised to get results in publication form sent straight to the composing rooms of the papers around the world. Good idea. Bad execution. For several days during the Games, it was abysmal. Lists of athletes set to compete were incorrect and late. Many of those who finished were shown with incorrect results. We finally had to resort to posting manually the starting lists and results. So much for high-tech. Even my alma mater, BellSouth, was having problems. Reuters, one of the heavy hitters among the IOC, was particularly furious at the company's inability to get service to them and for their explanations as to why they couldn't. Once we got them satisfied, then AP, the other heavy hitter, became unhappy with the lack of response to their phone service. When the press wasn't collectively berating us, we were all pointing our fingers at each other.

Three days into the Games, the media was calling us the Glitch Games because of the press technology not working as promised and for our transportation woes. One driver had gotten so fed up with the complaints from her passengers, that she stopped the bus, got off and was never heard from again. Another driver feared for his life when a press representative demanded to get off in the middle of the block and kicked the door out when the bus didn't stop. None of this seemed to bother the spectators who were having a great time and the television audience who was seeing spectacular competition, but it stressed the IOC because the press corps was stressed, and it stressed us because things seemed to be careening out of control. It took five days to finally get all the glitches fixed, not only the IBM results system, but our press transportation system as well. Once we did, the press calmed down. It had a tremendous impact on all of us, particularly Donna Johnsson who was working around the clock. We felt somehow we had let the organization down and had caused a lot of the bad press.

In retrospect, I should have left press operations where it was. I really didn't make it better by trying to supervise such a critical element of the

Games when my emphasis was somewhere else. By the time I focused on it, it was too late.

The paper took a good shot at me for the way the press operations ran and I couldn't disagree. If you accept the responsibilities, you accept the consequences.

While I found the general news coverage of the local media very uneven, I must commend the *Atlanta Journal Constitution*'s sports department. They left the whining and second-guessing to the newsroom and the columnists and covered the Games for what they were — the greatest sporting spectacle this city will ever witness. For a paper craving respect, the *Atlanta Journal-Constitution*'s sports coverage of the Centennial Games was as good as anybody's — maybe better.

I have taken a fair amount of criticism from the newspaper for the image that we projected to the world. I have thought long and hard about that in the perspective of the time that has passed. I should have toned down Billy's rhetoric. The Peter Ueberroth model was to keep expectations low and then when things went well, he looked like a hero. But that's not Billy. It was his unbridled enthusiasm that led him to believe that getting them for Atlanta was possible in the first place. I wasn't around when the deal was made that there would be no government backing for the Games, a pledge that the International Olympic Committee will never allow again. I was wrong to think that the city would be our partner. For that, I lay the blame squarely back on the newspaper's doorstep. Colin Campbell spent thousands of words trying to be farcical about Izzy being a Libyan agent and going off to Michigan or somewhere and getting a nose job (I'm not making this up). It was so bad that even the reporters confessed their embarrassment and bewilderment to me. While he was doing this, Atlanta was trying to hold us up for more money, crying racism when things didn't go their way, refusing to hire enough police or improve the morale of the ones they had, competing with us for marketing dollars. I once asked Bert Roughton why the paper wasn't putting pressure on the city to gets its act together. "That's not our job," he replied, "that's yours." They had time to worry about how Izzy looked, but not enough interest to worry about how the city looked.

Our transportation plan suffered because we couldn't get enough buses or enough drivers trained to drive them. We couldn't get the Atlanta police off their butts to direct traffic. The location of the park next door to our building put a crimp in the transportation plan because it forced us to relocate many of our routes. Yet, we moved millions of people successfully from venue to venue.

As stated earlier, the IBM results system was a severe problem for several days. We promised the media more than we could deliver. It was too complicated and untested. IBM took a hit in their image for their efforts but those of us responsible for the delivery of the service to the media must share also the blame. We didn't give the media what we had promised.

Where these problems damaged the image of Atlanta around the world, look no further than the "image-maker." The buck stops here. Maybe somebody more skilled than I would have whitewashed the problems as the city managed to do with the street vendor debacle, although I doubt it.

I have perhaps a different perspective. I make a lot of speeches around the country and I have yet to have someone come up to me afterwards and not tell me about the great time they had in Atlanta. They saw great competition, dealt with friendly volunteers, had no problem getting around town, and thought the Games were great. They either paid little attention to the newspapers or, if they did, they tended to discount the grumbling. It is their opinion that counts most.

The ones who were not here saw it on television and, true to Dick Ebersol's prediction, cared not that the city looked trashy, that the press was fussing, or if we could pay our bills. They tuned in for the competition and they got plenty of it.

Since 1996, the local paper has focused on Billy Payne's private records, the value of the memorabilia he sold, and his plans for a small museum at the Atlanta History Center to commemorate the 1996 Centennial Games. In doing so, they have managed to turn off most people in the city. To them, Billy is a hero and deserves better than he has gotten from the *Atlanta Journal-Constitution*. I am admittedly biased but the paper should be grateful for the good he did for Atlanta and encouraging him to take on The Next Great Project for a city in desperate need for one. I keep wishing they could be a catalyst for positive change, but I am reminded of how little influence they really have. Unfortunately, there are no more Ralph McGills around when we need them.

One of the familiar plaints of public relations people is that if there is another life after this one, most would like to come back as either a lap dog or a newspaper person. I don't like dog food so I chose newspapering instead.

I find it more than ironic that after thirty-five years of dealing with the media, I am now one of them. I am in my third year as a newspaper columnist. I write about politics and business issues for papers around the state and if my mail is any indication, I am developing a loyal following. I now call the public relations people for information as I was once called. I write things that infuriate companies as my company was once infuriated. I now harrumph just like all self-important columnists, assured that I am always correct.

And, yes, I second-guess and criticize. I guess it goes with the territory.

# 10

## LET THERE BE LIGHT

*The ceremony was just beautiful. You can't describe it.*
—Diary Entry, March 30, 1996

As glorious as the Olympic Games are with all the pageantry, celebration, and athletic competition, there is nothing that can compare to the Olympic torch relay. Like a flame applied to a combustible material, the torch ignites a tremendous burst of enthusiasm across the world unlike anything else connected with the Games.

I have been privileged to carry the torch twice—first in 1984 and again in 1996—and the experience is something I will carry with me for the rest of my life.

Contrary to what many people think, the torch relay is a relatively modern addition to the Olympic Games. In ancient Greece, the Olympic Games signaled a temporary halt to hostilities so that athletes could compete in peaceful competition. In the weeks leading up to the Games, heralds of peace—called *Spondophores*—ran through the villages of Greece announcing the Truce of the Gods and alerting the athletes to begin their trip to Olympia, the site of the Games. Tradition says the flame was born in a temple erected by the ancient Greeks to honor Hera, queen of the gods. The first flame appeared in the modern Games in Amsterdam in 1928 and again in Los Angeles in 1932.

It was in the 1936 Berlin Games that German professor Carl Diem carried the flame lighting one step further, suggesting a relay from Olympia across Europe and into Berlin to connect the Games' ancient traditions to the modern Olympic Games. It was a magnificent addition.

I knew we would have our work cut out for us after the outstanding torch relay of the Los Angeles Games in 1984. Peter Ueberroth, the LAOOC CEO, had ensured its success by getting AT&T to sponsor the event. The company put its management abilities—and its dollars—solidly behind the effort. Unbeknownst to anyone at the time AT&T signed up, the divestiture of the Bell System would occur before the relay would ever take place. The company was forced to manage the logistical challenge with seven new Baby Bells that the breakup had spawned. In spite of the upheaval, everybody worked extremely well together.

Runners could qualify to run with the torch or designate someone as a runner by paying $3,000 to a charity. For that, the participant would run a kilometer and keep the torch. As an employee, first of the Bell System and then of newly created BellSouth Corporation, I was asked to coordinate the relay through the Southeast and readily agreed. I had a good staff, particularly a young man name Gil Parrish, who was an organizational dynamo and would love handling the logistics. AT&T had already done the hard work—establishing the route, the logistics, the press coverage, security, etc. All I had to do was make sure nothing got screwed up in my territory. For my trouble I would get to run the torch in Atlanta. I had no idea how emotional it would be.

I chose to run my kilometer down Peachtree Street, past BellSouth's headquarters. Built in the early '80s, the building was the first new construction in what had been a rundown area of Atlanta. There were still some rough areas in the neighborhood and, as luck would have it, I was going to start my leg of the relay in just such a section. Logistics called for runners to be on site a couple of hours before the time scheduled to allow for the torch being early. Nobody wanted to contemplate the torch showing up and there being no one there to greet it. Thus, I was standing on a deserted street corner in my white shorts and singlet, directly across the street from a tavern that catered to motorcycle gangs.

It was hard to be inconspicuous in such a getup as mine and to my despair, I was spotted by a burly, bearded type in a leather jacket, who pointed me out to a similarly dressed biker friend. Both nodded and went inside the bar to get their friends. "I am a dead man," I told myself, "I will never live to run the torch." The bar emptied out and everyone was staring at me from across the street. Suddenly, one of the bikers grinned and yelled, "Go, USA." A roar erupted from the crowd as some of the toughest looking people I have ever seen cheered me and waved American flags. All I could manage was a weak smile and a feeble wave. They returned to the bar and later joined the thousands of others who had gathered on the street corner to see the flame come through Atlanta. By the time I finally received the torch at about 8:30 PM, the sidewalks were ten deep with people. It was going to be the same way in Atlanta. No doubt about it.

The plans for our torch relay were in the firm hands of Ginger Watkins. As I stated earlier, Ginger took a lot of gibes in the media for having come into her position at ACOG by having been one of the original members of the bid team and not for any particular skill as a manager. That was unfair to her. She was extremely well organized and had a great grasp of details. She came across to a lot of people as brusque and was not an easy person to work for, but when you look at the responsibilities she had in the organization, including the opening and closing ceremonies and the torch relay, Watkins hit a homerun on every assignment.

For all the clucking from the press about things that didn't work well in Atlanta, they conveniently forget the things that did, and they were all under the supervision of our own Steel Magnolia.

The logistics for the relay nearly rivaled those of the Games themselves. The Olympic Flame would be lit in Olympia at the end of March, would tour Greece, arrive on the shores of the United States on April 27, and then begin an eighty-four day, 16,700-mile relay through 3000 communities in forty-two states and within a two-hour drive of 90% of the U.S. population. That meant that someone had to get the torch block-by-city-block and mile-by-rural-mile across the country and keep it on schedule. It was one thing to plan the route but then someone had to be with the relay to ensure that everything worked as planned. That was the job of Watkins's able lieutenant, Hilary Hanson, and her team. A forty-vehicle caravan and 110 people were with the relay for the entire trip, distributing torches along the day's route, getting torchbearers shuttled to designated rendezvous points, keeping local communities up-to-date on the relay's progress and helping with details of some 500 local celebrations along the way.

The flame would travel by bus, cable car, pony express, train, ferry, sail boat, steamboat, wheelchair, bicycle, and, of course, by foot. Some

10,000 people from all fifty states would participate in the relay. Of that number, 5500 would be selected in their own communities as "Community Heroes," with the United Way helping make the selection. Eight hundred would be Olympians selected by the United States Olympic Committee. The Coca-Cola Company, which was the relay's presenter, would get 2,500 slots through its own Share the Spirit program in which consumers could nominate candidates. The rest belonged to ACOG.

The torch itself was a thing of beauty. It was thirty-two inches high and resembled the simple ancient torches—a gathering of reeds bound by twine. Designed by Peter Mastrogiannis, a graphic designer of Greek descent, the "reeds" of the torch represented each of the Modern Olympic Games and was bound in the middle by a handle of Georgia hardwood, donated by the Georgia Forestry Commission. The name of each Olympic Games host city was etched on a gold band near the base of the torch. A gold band above the handle featured the Atlanta 1996 logo.

As beautiful as it was, the flame had to be reliable and burn in all kinds of weather and under all kinds of conditions. Could the same people who had designed Izzy that caused all kinds of eye rolling and shortness of breath in the media actually make a torch that would work? The answer is yes. Georgia Tech professor Sam Shelton and Atlanta Gas Light Company engineer Vinton Wolfe provided us a flame that burned brightly and reliably for the entire relay.

As with anything Olympic, we had a few controversies to hurdle before the relay could begin. The first, of course, was whether to run the torch through Cobb County, home of the infamous "family values" resolution that had just lost an Olympic venue because of the county commission's unwillingness or inability to heal its own self-inflicted wounds. Moving the venue had cost the county money; not running the torch through the county would add insult to injury.

There was not as strong a division inside the organization on the issue of whether to route the relay through Cobb County as there had been earlier about moving the volleyball competition. Moving the venue was a logistical and financial decision; not running in Cobb County was symbolic. The Olympics Out of Cobb group had let it be known that they would harass the torch across the country if we did run in Cobb. They were threatening to block routes, raise hell, and even try to douse the flame with water. My wife, Jane, who has had to suffer through the slings and arrows of my career, was aghast that anyone would take something as beautiful as the torch relay and turn it in to a political issue. I had to agree with her but I had to be practical, too. Special interest groups are about special interests—theirs, not yours. You may not like them or what they do but that is not the point when you are in the external counseling business. You have to look at all the risks they pose and recommend to your management the correct action to take. Leave the personnel philosophy to somebody else.

The bigger issue was not to punish the citizens of Cobb County. There were a lot of good people who qualified as Community Heroes there and they deserved a chance to run the flame, too. It just might not be in Cobb County.

Our biggest problem was in getting the gay rights group to put on the muzzle. We knew what we wanted to do but we didn't need them fanning the flames. Jon Ivan Weaver, who seemed to be enjoying his fifteen minutes of fame, was telling everybody that he had it on "good authority" that we were going to run the torch through Cobb County and make an announcement on November 15 1995 to that effect. Nice going, except we wouldn't make a final decision on where the torch ran until spring of 1996. The media—which never met a rumor they didn't like—really were not buying his story. At the same time, we were beginning to pick up rumblings from the other side—particularly Congressman Bob Barr—that he wanted to see the torch run through Cobb.

Barr is an interesting guy. A former U.S. Attorney, he has developed a reputation in Congress as a hard right-wing, take-no-prisoners ideologue. In private, I found him reasonable and courteous. In a meeting with him at the end of December 1995, I explained the situation to him and the likelihood that unless the county commission showed some movement on the "family values" resolution, we probably weren't going to be able to justify running the torch through Cobb County. I guess I was expecting the kind of eruptions I had received from Gingrich but, instead, he was very understanding. He said he would try to do what he could to help but wasn't sure he could. As with Hillary Clinton later, you don't have to like somebody's politics to like the person. I like Bob Barr.

Some business people in Cobb County asked me how I rated the odds of the Olympic Flame going through the county. While it was not my decision to make, I rated the odds 5 to 1 — against. Actually, they weren't even that good. It was more like a snowball's chance in hell that the Olympic torch relay would come through Cobb County.

By March, we had made the decision and were just waiting for the Georgia legislature to get out of town. We sure didn't want to pull the plug while they were still in session and face some repercussions from our decision.

We announced that we were not running the torch relay through Cobb County on April 18, 1996, some ninety-two days before opening ceremonies and some eight days before the flame was to arrive in the United States. There was no sermonizing. Just a short statement saying that since the Cobb County commission had not changed its stance on the resolution that caused us to move the preliminary volleyball venue in 1994, we weren't going to run the torch through the county.

As with the move of the venue out of Cobb County, I called commission chairman Bill Byrne to tell him and he was not in the office. I faxed him our statement and he never called back. He was probably the least surprised person in the county and I suspect as glad to get rid of us as we were to get this behind us. Congressman Barr was once again a gentleman. He didn't agree with our decision, obviously, but wasn't going to make an issue of the move. I also called the governor's office and the offices of our two U.S. senators, Nunn and Coverdell, as well as some of the people in Cobb who had been supportive of us like Johnny Isakson and Matt Towery. The contacts had gone well.

In the meantime, I had asked Billy to call Gingrich. I had predicted to him that the Speaker would express some irritation and fuss a little bit but would probably want to use the conversation as an opportunity to lobby for some high-profile exposure during the Games.

Was I wrong.

If the Speaker had been irritated at our moving the venue out of Cobb a couple of years earlier, he went into overdrive over the torch relay decision. It was, he said, one of the worst decisions ever made. (This wasn't the time to tell him, but right off the top of my head I could think of two or three decisions over the centuries that might have topped this one.) Gingrich wanted to know how many dictators would be at the Games and how many countries would be in Atlanta that had dictators.

145

While we were trying to figure out what all of that meant, the Speaker told Billy he wanted to see him in Washington over the weekend to discuss the matter further. I called the Speaker's chief of staff to let him know that no amount of pressure from Gingrich would make us change our decision. I got a call in a few minutes saying the Speaker had cooled off and wasn't interested in having a meeting since we had already made our minds up. That worked out well. Billy Payne had already left to go play golf. He had earned it.

After the big blowup, Gingrich rarely mentioned the issue again. He was extremely gracious and supportive. You just had to withstand the initial storms and they weren't very pleasant.

There was also a minor dust-up about running in Prague and Yale, Oklahoma to honor the hometowns of the great American Olympian Jim Thorpe, hero of the 1912 Stockholm Games. We had not planned to go there but the locals made such a fuss about it, we relented. It was the right thing to do.

There was one other slight deviation in the relay route that bears a quick mention. Governor Miller called me one day as the torch neared Georgia. He sounded almost apologetic, which was not like the governor. He is a man who suffers fools poorly and could be extremely blunt. He had not been happy with ACOG since the early days because of our tendency to both over-promise and to talk about no government funding for the Games. He knew, and we knew, that the government would have to be involved — if not in the operations of the Games, which is what we meant — certainly in security matters. When I was first assigned government relations duties, it earned me a stern lecture from the governor and a set of expectations on what he wanted done and not done. I understood him loud and clear. Over the years, he began to soften toward us and, as I have said earlier, was a critical player in our efforts to secure government support for the Atlanta Games.

The governor on the telephone didn't sound like the governor who had given me that stern lecture a few years earlier. He went to great pains to say that he wanted no special favors. There was something he wanted me to look at and after I did, if there was any problem at all to drop it. He didn't even want a call back. His concern? The relay came close to his beloved hometown of Young Harris, in the North Georgia mountains. As the Olympic flame approached the town, the route veered and missed Young Harris altogether. Zell Miller was one of the most respected and influential governors in the country in 1996 but he was having trouble explaining to his sister why he couldn't get the torch to come through their hometown. Despite some grumbling from the planners, they agreed to change the route and run through Young Harris. I saw the governor a week or so later and he was very appreciative. He was back in his family's good graces again.

One of the things that Peter Ueberroth had had to contend with when AT&T agreed to sponsor the 1984 torch run was the IOC's fear that somehow the Olympic flame would be tainted through the association with the American corporation. Despite many well-founded criticisms of the commercialism of the Olympic movement, there is a clear recognition of where to draw the line. You will never see an advertising sign inside an Olympic venue, in spite of the fact that billions of people are watching on television. All venues have to be "clean." They certainly were not going to let the Olympic flame be exploited. Ueberroth had gotten around that by offering to have kilometers of the relay purchased for charity and AT&T was smart enough not to try and abuse their sponsorship of the event. Nonetheless, as he points out in his book, *Made in America*, his idea had enraged the Greeks. In fact, the International Olympic Committee and the Los Angeles Olympic Organizing committee had engaged in some skullduggery to sneak the flame from Olympia to the Chateau de Vidy in Lausanne, home of the IOC, in case the fractious Greeks refused to release it. (They later relented but Ueberroth had a spare flown from Lausanne, just in case.)

Their anger at Los Angeles organizers was nothing compared to the reaction in Greece when the 1996 Centennial Games were awarded to Atlanta. Many there felt the 100th anniversary of the modern Olympic Games was a divine right. After all, the original idea of the Truce of the Gods and the peaceful competition between warring city-states was theirs and the revival of the movement had occurred in Athens in 1896. To have the upstarts from Atlanta "steal" the prize from them could have been for only one reason: The Coca-Cola Company, whose world headquarters are in Atlanta and who has been a long-time sponsor of the Olympic movement. The company had to have been involved in the Games coming to Atlanta. Appropriate target, but wrong. Coca-Cola is sold worldwide and the last thing they want to do is to side with their hometown in a dispute that would cost them sales. One thing business understands is the bottom line and the bottom line to Coca-Cola was that they had more to lose than gain by supporting Atlanta. That didn't stop the Greeks from venting their frustration on the company and on the Atlanta organizers. We weren't going to make things easier because the lead "presenter" for our torch relay was to be — the Coca-Cola Company.

The Greeks are a passionate, argumentative, emotional group of people, at least the ones I met. When they argue with each other or with you, you are sure that a full-scale fight is about to break out. In the next minute, they will have you in an affectionate bear hug. I like them. They believe the Olympic movement is theirs. Somehow, it has gotten away from them and decisions are being made about something that is deep part of their culture by a group of people that they believe don't always share their passion.

One of the people who does is Billy Payne. As I have said a number of times, he was the only person I was to meet in my tenure at the Atlanta Committee for the Olympic Games who saw the real goodness of the Olympic movement. Some saw gold medals, some saw dollar signs, some saw marketing opportunities, some saw national glory. Some saw a loud speaker for their own special interest. Billy saw an opportunity for all the nations of the world — some of whom didn't even acknowledge the existence of other nations — to compete in a peaceful environment. A lot of cynics scoffed. The local paper snickered at his pronouncement that the Atlanta Games would be the greatest peacetime event of the twentieth century. But he was right and his critics were wrong. That is what the Olympic Games really are about. His beliefs were shared by the original band of Atlanta volunteers and they did a terrific job of winning back the friendship of the Greek Olympic officials, if not the Greek people themselves.

In early April 1995, many of us traveled to Athens to officially present the initial torch to Greek officials. First, we would attend the meeting of the Association of Summer Olympic Federations (ASOF) in Monte Carlo. This group represents the sports that appear in the Summer Games. Meetings were basically a gripe session. The federations fussed about tickets, accommodations, travel arrangements, the field of play and everything else they could think of. Most of their concerns fell to Dave Maggard, our managing director of sports. Some were serious concerns;

some were not. But ASOF was important and had to be listened to. No sporting federations, no Games.

While we had shown the torch to the executive committee of ASOF as a courtesy and had gotten good reviews, its design was still a secret. We were going to unveil the torch in simultaneous presentations in Athens and in Atlanta when we gave the first one to the Hellenic Olympic Committee. It was one of those good news stories that occur so infrequently in Olympic planning.

There was just one problem. We lost the torch.

Our group was gathered up in Monte Carlo and whisked by private limousines to Nice, France, where we were to board our flight for Athens. As with everything we did, meetings were going on right up to the minute of departure from the hotel. It meant packing and leaving in a hurry. Fortunately, we arrived in Nice in time to catch our breath for a few minutes and chat about the previous days' activities. As we relaxed, I made one of the few measurable contributions to the planning for the 1996 Olympic Games. I looked at Billy and asked, "Where is the torch?" Panic understates what followed. Frantically, we put in calls to the hotel in Monte Carlo to see if it had been left there. It had not. We called the transportation company that had driven us. They didn't have our torch.

We began retracing our steps in the airport and, happily, the torch lay where it had been left as we had moved from downstairs in the airport up to the lounge. Miraculously, it had not been spotted by security guards who might have thought it a bomb and blown it up. My reward for reminding my CEO that he had walked off and left the torch was his assigning to me the responsibility for its whereabouts from Nice until we presented it to the Greeks. I almost wore out the overhead compartment on the airplane on the trip to Athens, checking to see that it was still there. (While I was also responsible for dealing with external crises, I'm still not sure how we would have handled telling the Greeks, "You'll never guess what happened on our way to Athens. We lost the torch.")

The presentation of the torch was preceded by lectures from both Greek government officials and Hellenic Olympic Committee officials about giving Coca-Cola too big of a role in the torch run. But the fact that they even acknowledged a role for the company they loved to hate was remarkable. The thing they wanted most was for Billy to use his influence to persuade the IOC to award the next Games to Athens. In fact, they would get the 2004 Olympic Games.

Our presentation coincided with the 100th anniversary of the opening of the 1896 Games. We were treated to a concert in our honor and a grand fete hosted by the Minister of Sport that began at 12:30 AM and featured lots of food and wine. The entire day was a wonderful healing experience between two groups of people who feel strongly about the Olympic movement. As emotional and unpredictable as the Greeks can be, they treasure the Olympics and I will always have a very warm spot for Greece and its people.

Sometimes I think the Greeks were easier to deal with than Coca-Cola. A lot of the aura of the Olympic tradition eluded me, but I knew the corporate environment well, having survived three decades of it. The Coca-Cola company was a different animal than I had dealt with previously. As underwriter, or presenter, they would function much as AT&T had in 1984. There were two major differences. First, the runners would be selected in large part by local communities through the United Way and, second, we would handle most of the logistics ourselves, through the talents of Hilary Hanson and her right-hand man, Rennie Tritt.

Our plans were to announce the Coca-Cola Company's role at a news conference at Atlanta City Hall in February 1995. Scott Mall would write the news release and get sign-off from all parties, prior to the announcement. It was fairly straight-forward. Coca-Cola was going to be the presenter, United Way would provide volunteers and coordinate selection of those eligible to carry the torch and then we would throw in some factoids about the relay. At BellSouth, we were strong supporters of United Way. Our CEO, John Clendenin had been head of both the local Atlanta United Way as well as the national organization, and I knew from experience that any announcement that mentioned BellSouth and United Way would require a strong emphasis on the agency. But not at Coke.

I got a call from my public relations counterpart at Coca-Cola saying that we had United Way too far up in the lead of the release and they wanted them moved down in the story. Their reasoning was that United Way wasn't paying to underwrite the relay; the Coca-Cola Company was. I tried to explain that there was much to be gained by a soft positive release that talked about community volunteers and good deeds and the excitement of people across the country seeing the Olympic flame. But his hands were tied. His management wanted Coke to get the credit at the expense of their partners. As with all things negotiable, we worked out a compromise, but I never forgot the incident. They thought themselves omnipotent. They weren't. They were just insensitive to the external environment.

Part of their kitsch is to always have a bottle of Coca-Cola on the podium from which they are speaking. At City Hall, Ginger Watkins was busy coordinating the announcement and had her people scurrying around on the last minute details that crop up at events like this. Every time she looked up, somebody had placed a Coke on the podium. Ginger would order it taken down. It would be put back up. She would order it taken down. After the fourth time, she blew her stack. Even Coca-Cola realized there was a limit to what they could do. Nobody dared risk her wrath by placing the bottle on the stage a fifth time and the announcement went off without a hitch.

Another trauma was the intention of Hillary Clinton and Chelsea to attend the lighting of the flame in Olympia on the last day of March 1996. It is here that I must make a confession. I found Hillary Clinton much different than the one I had heard and read about. As I mentioned earlier, you don't have to like someone's politics to like that person. I didn't agree with Bob Barr's politics, but I liked him. I am sure the chairman of the Cobb County Commission, Bill Byrne, is not contemplating inviting me to dinner anytime soon, but I liked him. I found Jim Cherry, the chair of the Committee on Disabled Access, adversarial and much too political for my taste, but I liked him. And I liked Hillary Clinton.

My first exposure to her came when her staff called and said she wanted to attend the lighting of the flame in Olympia. It wasn't good news. The lighting of the flame in the Temple of Hera is a sacred moment to the Greeks and they were only going to invite a certain number of us to witness the event. The inclusion of the First Lady and First Daughter was sure to cause a media circus, some heavy-handed security measures by her Secret Service contingent and stress the members of the Hellenic Olympic Committee who made it clear it was their invitation that got you in to see the ceremony. Nobody else's. The administration had been talking to the Greek government about her attending but the government had no more influence with the Hellenic Olympic Committee than we did.

Billy was livid and wanted Charlie Battle and me to "uninvite" her. He felt it would detract from the symbolism of the lighting ceremony by having someone as high profile as Mrs. Clinton and Chelsea there. He was threatening not to attend himself if she came.

On the other hand, the administration was being very helpful to us and interested in our progress. Mrs. Clinton's chief aide, Melaine Verveer, was asking us why we were discouraging the First Lady's attendance. It was a good question without a good answer. Her staff promised that everyone was mindful of how special the lighting of the flame was to the Greeks and that they intended not to detract from the ceremony. Happily, things worked out well. She and Chelsea were well received.

The lighting of the flame was one of the most extraordinary experiences of my life. We arrived in Olympia on the Friday before the ceremonies on Saturday. We toured the area where the lighting was to take place. Walking down a hill, I came up on a flat area, smaller than a football field with a slab of marble embedded in the ground and running the width of the field. Standing on it, I asked my host what the marble was for. "That," he said, "is the starting line of the ancient Games." I was standing on the very spot that the athletes had stood some 2700 years earlier.

I will never forget that day. Before the ceremony, I was privileged to stand with Billy, A. D., Ginger Watkins, Linda Stephenson, Charlie Battle, Doug Bowles, Billy's friend and chief aide, and Hilary Hanson. We held hands, said a little prayer, cried a few tears of joy and then convened in the Temple for the lighting ceremony. To see the ceremony and not be distracted by the crowds in the stands was to be mentally transported back in time. It was eerie. This must have been the way it looked 2700 hundred years ago. It was breathtaking to watch the ceremony and the graceful women who conducted it and then to see the young Greek runner with the flame, headed out of the ancient stadium. It was the first step to Atlanta.

Even today, I look back on that trip to Olympia and say that all of the meanness and pettiness of Olympic Games planning was made bearable by that one incredible event. I still get emotional thinking about it.

Back home, we prepared for the Olympic flame to make its way to the United States and then across the country to Atlanta. Community heroes were being selected and each had a unique story of service to their community. We had planned not to announce their names until mid-February, but we got a call from President Clinton's office that he wanted to recognize two Community Heroes during his State of the Union message on January 23. How do you say no? We gave them a list of a dozen names and they selected Jennifer Rodgers, an Oklahoma City police officer who had helped rescue victims in the federal building bombing in 1995, and Lucius Wright, an educator from Jackson, Mississippi, who had worked in that city's anti-drug efforts. They were introduced to the world that night from the House gallery by the president who said they were not "star athletes. They are star citizens—community heroes meeting America's challenges, America's real champions." And there would be many more like them.

From the time the torch arrived in Los Angeles on April 27, the relay was an unqualified triumph. Every kilometer was a different but inspiring story. Crowds thronged along the route. Even Coca-Cola's efforts to plaster anything and everything with "Presented by Coca-Cola" signs couldn't detract from the celebration. A great source of pride to me was to see the Georgia State Patrol accompanying the flame in specially-provided BMWs. The stereotype of the southern state trooper as some pot-bellied, cigar-smoking redneck doesn't fit the GSP. These men and women are well conditioned and well trained. I am glad the rest of the country had a chance to see them, too.

I joined the torch relay in Little Rock on May 26 at the invitation of my friend, Mack McLarty. It was a compliment that he wanted me to come to his home state and be a part of the festivities and he hosted a nice reception for me on Sunday morning. It was an emotional day. I watched as the torch passed Central High School, the place where four decades earlier, President Eisenhower had used federal troops to integrate the school. One of those who had been involved in that trying time was now in a wheel chair and handed the torch off to a young white girl who had just graduated from Central. I looked around and everybody was crying: the runners, the mayor, Mack, the crowd. I noticed that I was crying, too. Somebody said later that the Olympic flame brought closure to that episode that had haunted Little Rock for too long.

The flame that left Little Rock on a special Union Pacific train and I looked at the number of people on the side of the tracks waving flags and applauding. It was amazing. That night, I joined Vice President Al

Gore in Memphis at a special celebration known as "May in Memphis." There were 60,000 people in attendance. I made a brief talk before the vice president and ad libbed my remarks. I was so pumped up over the day's activities that I didn't need a script. Not even for 60,000 of Al Gore's closest friends.

A week later, we had our first serious incident with the relay in — of all places — Indianapolis, Indiana. A group, identified as Black Panthers, burned an American flag and pulled a weapon on a stage manager. They were arrested.

The torch arrived in Washington, DC, on June 20. Several of us were invited to the White House where the torch would spend the night before continuing the journey to Atlanta. Prior to the festivities at the White House, we had a reception for the Georgia delegation at the Capitol, hosted by Newt Gingrich. After pulling the volleyball venue out of Cobb and not running the torch through the county — his district — I didn't know what to expect but he could not have been more gracious.

Since Jane had previously scheduled a week with her friends at our place on the Georgia coast, I brought my daughter Maribeth with me to Washington. A young woman with two children, it would be a once-in-a-lifetime experience for her. In fact, she had two experiences that I don't think either of us counted on and I'm not sure I ought to be talking about one of them even now.

After the reception for the Georgia delegation, we all freshened up and headed for the White House. One of the nice parts of the job had been my opportunity to have made a number of trips there, including several times in the Oval Office. But Maribeth had not seen it and neither had Martha Payne. Betty Curry, President Clinton's secretary, invited us in to look around the room. Billy was acting as host. "Martha," he said, "you see those high back chairs?" pointing across the room from the president's desk, "that's where Ronald Reagan used to fall asleep." Turning to my daughter, Billy said, "Maribeth, get our pictures sitting in the chairs." By now, Betty's smile was frozen and she was politely suggesting that pictures shouldn't be made unless authorized. Something about security risks. Big security risks. But that didn't stop Billy. He was lining us all up for photos in the Oval Office, including Ms. Curry. Maribeth is as cool as they come but I think she had visions of the Secret Service swooping into the room and confiscating her camera and getting us all arrested. But she kept clicking away. Once the photos were finished, Billy walked over to the president's desk, tried on the University of Arkansas NCAA championship basketball ring that had been presented to Clinton earlier and found it a perfect fit. With that, we left, much to the relief of a terror-stricken secretary and an amateur photographer who wondered what she had gotten herself into.

Her second unique experience occurred the following morning. The torch left the grounds of the White House when President Clinton handed the torch to Carla McGhee, a member of the United States women's basketball team who had been so severely injured just a few years earlier that it was not certain she would ever walk again, let alone play basketball.

After the ceremony, the president invited Governor and Mrs. Miller, Bob and Anne Holder, Billy and Martha Payne, Maribeth and me back in the White House, much to the consternation of his handlers who had him tightly scheduled. As they stood on one foot and the other, we engaged in a very informal conversation. I mentioned to Mrs. Clinton that Maribeth had enjoyed her book, It Takes A Village. My daughter proceeded to mention some things she had read in the book, which indicated to the First Lady that she had, in fact, read the book. With that, Mrs. Clinton engaged Maribeth in conversation about raising children and what it was like having a teenager in the family. Maribeth talked about her own two. Right before my eyes, I was watching two mothers talk about raising their children. Not once did the First Lady look around the room to see who else was there or what else was going on. It was a sincere and straightforward dialogue that went on for quite awhile. It was an extraordinary courtesy extended to my daughter. I don't know what goes on at the White House on a day-to-day basis and I don't really care. All I know is how nice Hillary Clinton was to Maribeth and I will never forget that.

As the torch neared Atlanta, the gay rights issue reared its head again. This time in South Carolina. In May, the Spartanburg County commission passed a resolution like Cobb County's and dared us to do anything about it. We were headed straight down the Atlantic seaboard and a detour at this point would be a logistical nightmare. A carpetbagger from New York had browbeaten the commission into

155

passing the resolution and then proceeded to excoriate us for pandering to gays, promoting the gay lifestyle, etc.

It was if the *Atlanta Journal Constitution* had died and gone to heaven. They had me in a wonderful bind. I had said earlier that we couldn't be the moral arbiter for the whole country. We would have every special interest group in the world holding us hostage over something. The only thing we could control was our own backyard and that included Cobb County. If we bypassed Spartanburg, weren't we acting like the politically-correct organization we said we were not going to be? If we planned to run through Spartanburg County, why not run through Cobb County? Wasn't that hypercritical? Reporters live for these kinds of moments.

The only thing to do was to get the resolution rescinded and hope there were people more willing to admit a mistake than there were in Cobb. We did. Or at least, the U.S. Gymnastics Federation did. They were scheduled to train there and there was no way they would do that with such a resolution in place. Also, I think the BMW facility that had located there also got involved. As a result, the commission changed their minds and voted to rescind their previous action.

Before we could congratulate ourselves on our success, the same guy that stirred the trouble in Spartanburg went twenty miles down the road and got the Greenville County Commission to pass the same resolution, 9-3, make the same threats and give us the same working over. Only this time, they let it be known that unlike their cousins to the north, there would be no backing down. The *Atlanta Journal Constitution*, which had devoted hundreds of column inches on why we needed to get out of Cobb County, was now criticizing us for being too hard-line the other way.

We had one thing working in our favor. Time was running out on the days until the Centennial Games were to begin. It frankly didn't matter what we did because there would be scant time for reprisals from either side (unless we decided to extend the Games a couple of weeks to get all the protests in). So we decided to lay low. Greenville County was thumbing its political nose at us, while the city of Greenville was planning one of the biggest celebrations we had experienced since the torch left Los Angeles a couple of months earlier. Should we bypass the county and punish the city? (The commission member from the city had voted against the resolution.) Should we be inconsistent and run through the county in order not to penalize the city? Speaker Gingrich had assailed us again for not running in Cobb County. He did, however, call Billy Payne and suggest that he be put in the same box with President Clinton, IOC president Samaranch, the governor, and the mayor. He thought that with three Democrats in the box, it might look better to have at least one Republican there, too. I told my friend, Billy, that there was a good political lesson to learn from that phone call. There's nothing so disagreeable between us that can't be overcome if two billion people can see me on television.

The Greenville decision was one of my favorites. We decided to put the flame in one of our caravan vehicles and bus it straight through the county without stopping. When we got to the Greenville city limits, we stopped, got the flame out and began the torch relay through town. I am told that the celebration in Greenville was one of the best of all and that the county commission was livid. I hope so.

From there it was clear sailing into Atlanta and the enthusiasm and excitement seemed to increase daily. A number of reporters ran in the torch relay and despite all the cynicism they had learned in journalism school, could not contain themselves as they reported on their own experiences. Among all the great stories about running with the Olympic flames, there were two that stood out because of my affection for the participants. First, Andrew Young, who had been on the front line of the civil rights movement and suffered unimaginable prejudice as a result, ran the torch across the Edmund Pettys bridge in Selma, Alabama. Billy Payne ran down the middle of Sanford Stadium at the University of Georgia, with his daughter, Elizabeth, and his son, Porter. He stopped at the point where his late father had sat and watched him play football and saluted his dad. From there, he handed the torch off to his coach, Vince Dooley.

As for me, I ran my relay in Cartersville, Georgia, the town where my mother had been born. Since I had run with the Olympic torch in Atlanta in 1984, I had gained a son-in-law and a daughter-in-law, and four grandsons. My son Ken and my son-in-law Ted escorted me over my route as the rest of the family cheered and took photographs. It was an unbelievable evening.

The Olympic flame had been on a long journey since that day in March when it had left Olympia. That journey would end on July 19 in our new stadium with the lighting of the cauldron. The trip had been filled with magical moments from one end of the country to the other and symbolized everything that is good about the Olympic movement.

It had also energized the nation. The planning period was over. Finally, it was time to let the Games begin.

# 11

## THE 1996 CENTENNIAL OLYMPIC GAMES

*All the mean spiritedness, all the politics, all the special interests are over-
arched by the pure goodness of the Games.*
—Diary Entry, July 19, 1996

The day had finally arrived: July 19, 1996. The beginning of the Games of
the XXVI Olympiad. It was difficult to explain the feeling you have after
the years of disputes, controversies, fears, and doubts to know that the
moment that we had all been working for was finally here. I was a
relative newcomer. I had joined the team in January 1993. I can only
imagine what this time must have been like for Billy, Charlie Battle,
Ginger Watkins, and Linda Stephenson. As a part of the original
volunteers, they had worked diligently to win the bid and then had
spent the past five years in key roles inside the organization to plan the
details. They had given almost ten years of their lives getting to this
moment.

But this was not the time to be reflective. The success or failure of the
Games would be determined by how we performed, not how we
planned to perform. We were ready.

The organization had grown from the original ten volunteers to over
100,000, with over half that number being volunteers. Billy Payne had
said all along that the Atlanta Games would be defined by the way we
treated our volunteers and, as usual, he was correct. There really is such
a thing as Southern Hospitality. As I have traveled around the country
since the Games, I have heard numerous positive stories about how
friendly people were in Atlanta. A big part of that was due to the ACOG
volunteers. Linda Stephenson and her staff had done a superb job of
volunteer training. Previous experience had indicated that as the

excitement wore off the Olympic Games and tedium set in, it was not unusual for the volunteer force to shrink considerably before the Games were over. Many volunteer jobs were not glamorous. A lot of them were just plain hard work. But there was no noticeable drop off in Atlanta. The volunteers seemed as enthusiastic at the end as they had when the Games began. They were the real heroes of 1996.

As the Olympic flame made its way across the country, we were busy making final preparations for its arrival and for the Olympic Games. Time was running short to get our burgeoning list of issues resolved. We had finally settled our dispute with the disabled. We had gotten our funding from the Department of Defense in spite of John McCain's incessant rantings.

The newspaper, as usual, was on top of its game. As we were finalizing our plans, they reported that Atlanta was the murder capital of the country and for once, they did set the standard for coverage around the world. The story was big news everywhere. It was not the way you wanted to welcome the world. Trouble is, it wasn't true. They had to run a retraction, saying the numbers they had put out were not accurate.

Maybe they had been inspired by our Attorney General Michael Bowers, who had his eyes on the governor's job. He was a darling of conservatives and of the media—an unusual combination. In the midst of questioning why Billy Payne needed state-provided security he had time to announce in March that it was safer to walk the streets of Sarejevo than the streets of Atlanta. We were just getting help from everywhere.

A red flag was going up over our transportation plans. We were over budget in that area and yet the plan had some major problems. We were even thinking about giving the whole issue to the state Department of Transportation and letting them run it.

Fifty-seven days before the start of the Centennial Games, Billy Payne went into the hospital to have surgery to repair a ruptured disc in his neck. This was his second hospitalization in three years but was not as serious as his heart surgery. He would be required to be in a soft cast for a few weeks and, thankfully, the media coverage was fairly benign.

We had opened our new stadium with the U.S. Track and Field Grand Prix and things had gone well although it was hot as blazes, raising the question of what the weather would be like two months hence.

We were in the "last of everything" phase—last ACOG board meeting, last MAOGA meeting, last IOC Coordination Commission meeting. As with all Olympic Games cities, the IOC appoints a group of members and federation representatives to monitor all of the activities of the local planning committee and to advise and counsel on your progress. The Atlanta Coordination Commission was headed by Dick Pound, a Canadian and a member of the IOC's powerful executive committee. They could ask hard questions based on their experiences and they had done so over the past five years. However, they were feeling good about where we were in our planning. For a change, they were more optimistic than we were inside. Finances were going to be very tight. With less than a month to go, we were still some $12-15 million short. Not bad for a $1.7 billion budget but still serious. The big question was, if we had to cut where would it be? Billy had made it clear that the ceremonies would not be touched and you could understand his logic. After all, that would be one of the most viewed events of the entire Olympic Games. The cuts would have to come from somewhere else. Like the other departments, I was having trouble defending the press's turf from A. D. Frazier's budget cutters.

Kevin Gosper, a member of the IOC executive committee and an Australian, was the Coordination Commission member with oversight for press operations. He had expressed concern about the transportation arrangements. The space across the street from our building had been intended as the primary pickup and drop-off point for the press since the Main Press Center was located in our building. The creation of Centennial Olympic Park had dealt that plan a serious blow. Now press would be shuttled between the MPC and a parking lot some thirteen blocks away.

Also, we were being assured constantly by IBM that their technology system would be up and running when the world press arrived. Writers would have a wealth of information at the touch of a screen on any aspect of a particular sport or athlete. Turns out that what they really wanted were starting information and results.

The press was beginning to complain about the distance from the field to the interview areas. In some cases, it was a long walk and they weren't used to being inconvenienced. I found myself constantly at odds with Manolo Romero, who was a strong advocate for the television journalists, as he should have been. Manolo reminded us many times of how much money the broadcasters were putting into the Games. The obvious insinuation was the press was a cost-causer and if there was a conflict on sight lines or seats or conveniences, the emphasis should be on satisfying the broadcasters. Doug Arnot, who had been brought in from the World Cup as venue manager, was a solid guy. He was also prone to remove a few press seats for other purposes. There were not two better people at ACOG than Arnot and Romero, but tempers were getting frayed as time grew short. It was ironic because when Arnot joined us in 1994, one of the reporters at the *Atlanta Journal Constitution* predicted a turf war between Manolo, Doug, and me. We had all been amused at the time, but now we weren't laughing. There were only so many seats to go around and the question was, whose seats were they? There was no question who ran the venues. Doug Arnot did. He had the power to giveth seats or taketh away. We were all lobbying him for our fair share.

While trying to get issues resolved with our Department of Defense requests and help bring the ADA issues to a close, I was also trying to help Donna Johnsson and our people defend the press arrangements at the Games. I needed to be two or three people.

In spite of everyone's angst, things seemed ready. Centennial Olympic Park opened on July 13. The Athletes' Village was opened. The Main Press Center and the Welcome Center at the Airport were also ready. Some 5000 banners were hung around town. Athletes were arriving daily as were members of the media. Sponsor hospitality tents were up and running.

It was time for the Opening Ceremonies.

The choice of Don Mischer to produce the opening and closing ceremonies was one of the best decisions that the organization had made. Every job has its own pressure. In fact, there were few jobs at ACOG that weren't packed with pressure. But try this: Get 10,000 dancers, singers, baton twirlers, bands, and choirs, young and old. Put them in elaborate costumes. Get them to perform a mind-boggling array of music and drama in perfect precision for three hours. Throw in plenty of flags, fireworks, thirty chrome trucks, and a salute by the U.S. Air Force Thunderbirds. March in 10,000 athletes in the middle of the show. Have two billion people watching and do it live. That is how I define pressure. To Don Mischer and his chief aide, David Goldberg, it was all in a day's work. Mischer's credits included producing the Emmy

Awards, Broadway's Tony Awards, Irving Berlin's 100th birthday celebration, Super Bowl halftime shows, and specials on Mikhail Baryshnikov, the Pointer Sisters, Bob Hope, and Willie Nelson.

You would expect someone who works under that kind of pressure to be a temperamental, high strung, headset-throwing screamer. Not Mischer. He was low key and one of the nicest people I worked with. I marveled at how matter-of-factly he and Goldberg planned the opening ceremonies extravaganza. I would have been a basket case trying to do what they did; yet, one day Mischer came into my office to thank me after I had deflected a media issue off of him and expressed relief that he didn't have the pressure of dealing with the media as I did. It's all in the eyes of the beholder.

The biggest secret of the Games was who would light the cauldron in the opening ceremonies. Despite the intense interest and the fact that ACOG was worse than government for leaks, this one amazingly held. I had known for several months as had several others who had a need to know. Billy Payne's secret was safe with me. Someone once marveled at how I never gossiped or told secrets. "That," Jane said, "is because he can't remember what you told him five minutes later." She was right but this was one secret that I wouldn't forget. I thought the selection of Muhammad Ali was outstanding.

The choice had been influenced by Dick Ebersol, president of NBC Sports. Initially, plans were for runners to scale the steps of the 116-foot high steel tower holding the cauldron and cross a 190-foot long bridge. Atop the structure was a sixteen-foot tall stainless steel cauldron, trimmed in red Georgia clay. The structure had been designed by noted sculptor Siah Armajani. As runners progressed up the steps, it would build excitement until the cauldron would be lit and the Centennial Games would begin.

But it wasn't good television.

It would be hard to see the runners going up the steps because of the structure. It was better to come around the track in the traditional manner and then light the torch. But how and by whom? There again, Ebersol had a candidate. Why not Muhammad Ali? After some deliberation, Payne agreed.

On opening night, large screens inside Olympic Stadium kept the crowds apprised of the location of the torch relay and the anticipation building. Four-time Olympic gold medallist Al Oerter passed the flame to three-time heavyweight champion (and Atlantan) Evander Holyfield. Holyfield entered through a tunnel under the stadium and up on a platform in the middle of the field to a thunderous ovation. As he made it on to the track, he was joined by Voula Patoulidous of Greece, in what was one of my favorite memories of the 1996 Games. After the squabbles and hurt feelings between Atlanta and Greece over the awarding of the Centennial Olympic Games to Atlanta, here were an American and Greek athlete carrying the flame together. Having been there at the lighting of the flame in Olympia, I found this a special gesture of friendship. On the other side of the track, Holyfield and Patoulidous handed the flame off to U.S. gold medal swimmer Janet Evans and she climbed a ramp toward the cauldron and then stopped and lit the torch of Ali. When the crowd realized who he was, there was an audible gasp and then a mighty roar. It was one of the most electric moments I have ever witnessed. Ali, his hands shaking from palsy, lowered the torch to ignite a special flame that propelled up a long cable to the cauldron. Maybe nobody else saw it, but as the torch began to move up the cable, it seemed to hesitate for just a split-second. That was the longest split-second in my life. Then it resumed the journey and the cauldron burst into flame.

It had been a grand and glorious night. One tragedy occurred that night with the death of a Polish Olympic official who suffered a heart attack on the field. But the Games were underway. Now all we had to do was make it through the next seventeen days and the Centennial Olympic Games would be history.

We all got home about 3:00 AM and were back at the office three hours later, still on a high from the Opening Ceremonies. Now it was the athletes' turn. The athlete is the number one constituency of any Olympics. Without them, there are no Games. You must get them to their assigned venue on time and with as little stress as possible and then return them to the Athlete's Village when they are through. Most have trained all their lives for this moment and they don't need any distractions. One of Billy Payne's strongest admonitions to the staff was that every athlete at our Games was an Olympian, whether they won a gold medal or finished last on their first effort and were eliminated. They were all special and deserved our very best efforts.

We began each day during the competitions with a 6:00 AM meeting to talk about problems we were having and what we planned to do to solve them. In attendance were all of the managing directors and other subject matter experts, as needed. We looked at weather reports, scheduled competitions, attendance, traffic flow, security concerns, concessions, and anything else. From there, several of us made the daily trek to the Marriott Marquis, where we would get the IOC's assessment of the previous day's activities and their concerns. This would be our "to do" list for that day and we would report back to them the next morning on our progress.

It is easy to lose perspective when you are working eighteen-hour days and you are dealing with problems. From what I could see and hear, the athletes were spectacular and the fans were having a great time. In the meantime, we were dealing with our transportation system and our technology results system. The transportation system was the IOC's concern as well. Because of the traffic around their hotel, members were having a hard time getting to where they wanted to go. Our police department sure wasn't making much effort to solve the problem. This was impacting not only the IOC members, but the members of the media who were trying to get from the Main Press Center at Inforum and the International Broadcast Center just down the street to the venues.

The Marriott Marquis overlooks the downtown connector, which consists of I-75 and I-85. On a normal business day, you can expect to see traffic completely stopped on that portion of the connector. For the seventeen days of the Games, the interstate looked almost deserted. For that, we can thank the Metropolitan Atlanta Rapid Transit Authority (MARTA), the very clean and efficient system that runs from the suburbs to Atlanta. The system was operating twenty-four hours a day with extra rail cars and buses. For many Atlantans, it was their first experience to ride MARTA and, unfortunately, as soon as the Games were over, most went back to their cars and clogged the freeways again.

Granted, it took MARTA a day or two to get the kinks out because of the numbers of riders but they quickly got on top of the situation and by the time the Games were over, they had carried over seventeen million passengers.

I wish the press technology had done as well. It was clear when the Games began that the IBM results system technology was not reliable. Members of the media were getting incorrect information on upcoming competitions and then results that were not always accurate. We spent the first day almost exclusively trying to get the IBM system to work.

Every day, it would seem to be getting better and then something would happen that would let us know it was still not functioning as promised.

By the third day, the press was in a state of rebellion. The technology wasn't working well and neither was their transportation system. If you think the press is fair and unbiased, screw up their information system and their transportation and see how impartial they are. Few papers, as I recall, were saying, "Hey, we are having big time problems, but the fans seem to be having a great time and the competitions are superb." Many members of the press were calling the Games a disaster.

In the meantime, the athletes were still doing great, the people were having a good time, our venues were full, Doug Arnot and his people were moving the crowds in an out of the stadiums in a timely and efficient manner, the weather was perfect, and Centennial Olympic Park was full of celebrants. While all of this was going on, A. D. Frazier was meeting with the city of Atlanta and the Georgia Department of Transportation, trying to get someone to direct traffic around the downtown area and not having much luck.

Street vendors were finally coming to the conclusion that they were going to take a bath financially. The promise of untold riches was gone and so were their customers. They were threatening to demonstrate—not against Munson Steed, the architect of the ill-fated program—but against ACOG. They had clogged up our streets with their sheds, impeded traffic flow downtown, made us look like a back alley in Algiers and they wanted to blame us. Our cup runneth over.

Kevin Gosper was trying to get the press mollified. He wanted the results system fixed or scrapped. He showed us a list of people who had set swimming records and many of them were listed twice. A. D. and I were hauled before a representative group of press and listened to them complain about transportation and the technology. We thought we had both fixed until there was a major breakdown of the technology system that afternoon. We were in our fourth day.

The Europeans Broadcast Union and NHK, the Japanese broadcasting network, was threatening to file suit over the poor quality of the information system. To say that Manolo Romero was an unhappy camper was an understatement. I was going to retire when this was all over. He had to face the same people again at the next World Cup.

I had received tickets to a number of events as had the other members of the management team. Of course, getting to see any Olympic competitions was out of the question until we could get the glitches fixed. In the meantime, my son Ken and daughter Maribeth were attending events with my grandsons and friends and were having a blast. They would call to tell me how easy it was to get to the events, how efficient getting through security checkpoints was and how great the competitions were. From where I sat, it sounded like they were at another Olympic Games somewhere. "Come on out, Dad," Maribeth told me on the phone one day, "it is great." "Can't do it," I replied, "I've got too many problems to deal with."

By the fifth day, Billy was doing a number of interviews with the media talking about how great the Games were going and apologizing for the technological glitches and the transportation woes downtown that were impacting them. A. D. was losing his patience with IBM. He told the local paper that the technology problems lay squarely at the feet of IBM. "They say the problem is fixable," an exasperated Frazier told the *Atlanta Journal-Constitution*, "I don't know why it wasn't fixable before now."

I had worked in big business long enough to know that sometimes the only way to get something fixed is to have the CEO say, "Fix it." Of course, that can't occur if the people in the organization are hiding the problem from him. In the case of IBM, the issue was out there for everybody to see. To make matters worse, the company had hyped the system prior to the Atlanta Games and had everybody's expectations that it was a technological marvel. When the time came to produce, we couldn't even tell the media who was starting where and how they did when they finished.

Finally, somebody got the attention of Lou Gerstner, IBM's CEO, at what the furor was doing to his company's image. It surely wasn't me. In my one effort to get him involved, I called one of the IBM public relations people who told me that the chairman was busy entertaining customers. When he did get involved, he fixed the problems. I am told that he got everybody in a room and read them the riot act. Sounds like something a CEO with a problem of this magnitude would do but, regardless, the technology issue was finally resolved. But it had taken too long and the damage had been done. Two years later, as they readied for the Winter Games in Nagano in 1998, news reports said, "IBM is trying to rebound from the embarrassing worldwide scrutiny it received during and after the 1996 Olympic Games in Atlanta." They later announced that, for financial reasons, they were through with the Olympic Games. Their performance in Atlanta had tarred IBM and it had tarred us, too.

By the sixth day, things were improving noticeably. It was like a second wind. On July 24, the track and field competitions began and those, despite the protestations of the other federations, are the glamour events of the Olympic Games. There would be morning sessions and evening sessions at Olympic Stadium concurrent with baseball competitions at Atlanta-Fulton County Stadium just across the parking lot. Baseball competition was popular because these games offered the cheapest tickets to the Olympic Games and meant a family of four could attend for less than $25. The result was that the operations people would be moving a quarter of a million people in and out of the stadiums twice a day for eight days in an area less than a mile square.

Our technology people were working with Associated Press to develop a backup system to the one that had been designed to send results back to the papers in a printable format.

Television viewing was breaking records. In the two most recent days, we had sold 70,000 walk-up tickets, meaning that people were buying tickets on the spot to a future competition. While we were impartial, it didn't hurt that the Americans were doing extremely well in the Games.

The media was finally turning positive. On Wednesday, Billy had lunch with editors from the top news organizations and was candid in assessing the problems, but refused to get caught up in the controversy with the City of Atlanta vending program. "I have been out on the streets," he said, "and it looks like everybody is having a good time." The luncheon got him some good press. A. D. also did a news conference and, although it was not well attended, that was a good sign. If the media were out for blood as they had been in the first few days, they would have been there *en masse* to do battle with him over the operations of the Games. Even the IOC seemed a little more kindly disposed to us. Maybe they had given up on Atlanta's ability to direct traffic.

President Clinton and his family came on the July 25 and this held up competition for about an hour because they were late and because of the increased security, but there were few complaints. The same thing the next day when Al Gore came to town. Finally, things were running as we had hoped they would. We were half way home, everybody seemed happy and I was even contemplating sneaking out to one of the venues with my family. I wanted to share the Olympic experience with my grandsons, whom I had not seen since the start of the Games a week earlier. This was the way I had imagined the Olympic Games when I signed on in 1993.

Then, the bomb exploded in Centennial Olympic Park. Our days were about to become more difficult than any of us could ever have imagined.

I have talked previously about how we handled the bombing strategically, but beyond the strategies was the response of the people. Our crowds were as large as ever, the media—while on a feeding frenzy over who did it—seemed almost sympathetic to a group of people they had savaged only a few days earlier. I remember talking to Melissa Turner at the *Atlanta Journal Constitution* hours after the bombing. We had done daily battle and would do more but for that one moment, we were sharing our grief with each other. It is the only time I cried during the experience.

I was getting calls from friends around the world who had seen the news on television. I learned the power of television following the bombing. Randy Burgess was a student at the University of Georgia and the son of a good friend on St. Simons Island, Georgia, where we have a second home. His father was in Hong Kong watching CNN when he learned of the explosion. He immediately called his son in Atlanta to see if he was okay. Randy was asleep and unaware of what had happened. His dad instructed him to call his mother, 300 miles away and let her know that he was safe. She, too, did not know the bombing had occurred. They were informed of the bombing from halfway around the globe, thanks to television news.

There is nothing funny about tragedy, but I remember two lighter moments. The first occurred on July 30 when the Atlanta paper published an Extra, announcing that the lead suspect in the bombing was Richard Jewell. Television's instant coverage of news had made the press's interest in publishing an extra edition to cover a major news story a thing of the past. I was amazed. I had not seen an extra edition of a newspaper in perhaps forty years. I told a couple of my staff members,

"You won't believe it but the *Atlanta Journal Constitution* has just published an Extra." I could see from the blank stares that they had no idea what I was talking about. I was dealing with the television generation.

The second example of humor in tragedy happened on the Saturday night before the end of the Games. There were a number of senior managers who were in constant radio contact with each other twenty-four hours a day. If you got to bed, you put the radio right beside you. It was the most critical communications channel we had. I was at home when I got a message from Doug Arnot that there was a strong likelihood that another bomb had been found. We had had hundreds of bomb threats and evacuations since the park bombing but this one looked to be the real thing because one of the bomb-sniffing dogs had made a "hit" on it. As I was preparing to return to the office, Doug came back on the radio and said that, happily, it was a false alarm. The dog was mistaken.

Months later I was recounting this story in a speech when someone asked me, "What happened to the dog?" I was taken aback by the question because I hadn't really thought about it, but I felt the questioner deserved a reply. "We took the dog," I replied, "to the Grand Canyon, showed him a stick, threw it in the canyon and said, 'Fetch, boy.'" (Note to all animal lovers: I was only kidding.)

With Centennial Park reopened, things got back to as normal as a catastrophe in such a huge event would allow. While the media chased their tails and Richard Jewell, some were beginning to wonder if, in fact, he really was the prime suspect.

We had to remember there were Games still going on. Michael Johnson electrified the world with a double win in the 200 and 400 meter races, the first person to ever do so. Dot Richardson, a thirty-five-year old aspiring doctor, hit a home run that won the gold medal for the women's fast pitch softball team and then boarded a plane for California, to assist in surgery. She was one of the great stories of the Atlanta Games. The U.S. women won the gold medal in soccer on the field at Sanford Stadium before some 80,000 fans, the largest crowd to ever see a women's soccer game. On the not so pleasant side, Dick Pound's wife was arrested for disobeying a police officer and resisting arrest. I found the Atlanta police department's sudden interest in enforcing the traffic laws of the city commendable, but a tad late.

The years have clouded a lot of the bad memories of the Centennial Games and have allowed me to remember the special things. Running the torch in my Mother's hometown with my son and son-in-law. Seeing the flame lit in the special ceremony in Olympia. Watching the people of Little Rock gather in front of Central High School and celebrate their future. Witnessing the Opening Ceremonies. Meeting a lot of wonderful people around the world.

On the last night of the competitions I had another wonderful experience. I had grown up in East Point, just south of Atlanta. All my life, I had known Fred Alderman there. He was in our church and my future wife and I went to high school with his daughter, Lucy. Years later, I had joined Southern Bell Telephone Company and was assigned the responsibility of visiting with AT&T shareowners in their homes to bring them up-to-date on their investment and to answer any telephone services questions they might have. I had chosen Mr. Alderman as one of the owners to visit. He was a polite and dignified man and I knew he would be pleased to see that I was surviving in the corporate world.

I called on him and we had a pleasant conversation. He excused himself to leave the room and as I waited for him to return, I casually thumbed through a book on the end table entitled, *Amsterdam Olympics*. I was dumb-founded to see his picture on one of the pages with three U.S. teammates, with the caption, "4x400 gold medal winners." I had known Fred Alderman all my life and didn't know he had won an Olympic gold medal. Forget the shareholder visit. When he returned, I was almost too excited to talk. Yes, that was him and, yes, he had won a gold medal and, no, he wasn't quite sure where it was. He believed it to be upstairs. From that moment on, Fred Alderman was my hero. As the years passed, I would see him occasionally at my old church. When I joined the Atlanta Committee for the Olympic Games, I promised him that he would see the 4x400 relay as my guest. When the time came, Mr. Alderman was in a wheel chair (although he had carried the torch during the relay) and I had reserved a suite for him and his family. I had found out over the years that he had been the NCAA sprint champion at Michigan State and was in the school's hall of fame. I brought IOC member Kevin Gosper by the suite to meet Fred Alderman, since Kevin had won a silver medal in the 1956 Melbourne Games and had also attended Michigan State.

What I wasn't prepared for, however, is that the Alderman family had located the other living member of the gold medal team from 1928.

His name was George Beard, from Armonk, New York, and as luck would have it, he had handed the baton to Mr. Alderman. There was a picture of that exchange taking place in Amsterdam. The family had invited Mr. Beard to the box to sit with their dad. The two men had not seen each other since getting off the boat in New York sixty-eight years earlier. Now, they were together again. It was a magical moment.

I had thought of this night through the stressful times that had preceded it and felt somehow responsible for entertaining Fred Alderman. He didn't want to be entertained. He wanted to watch the race. With his teammate from 1928 sitting next to him, I watched the years lift from two old men (Mr. Alderman was now ninety; George Beard, eighty-eight) as they followed the athletes around the track. Both seemed to be running the race in their minds and I noticed they slightly leaned into the turns as the runners did. To put an exclamation point on the evening, the U.S. runners won the gold medal, just as they had in 1928. It was on the last night of the competitions and I had kept my promise to my hero. Not a bad way to end.

The next night was Closing Ceremonies and I had wondered often how I would deal that night. I am not a nostalgic person, but I knew that I would be sitting with people that I would never see again. People that I had fought with, laughed with, schemed with, and who I had spent more time with than my own family over the past three-and-a-half years. What would it be like when the flame was extinguished and it was finally over? Interestingly, I felt nothing. When it was all over, I simply gathered up my wife and kids and we went home. No tears. No sad farewells. No memorable moments. As impressive as the Closing Ceremonies were (Don Mischer had done his magic again), they were anticlimactic after all we had been through. The evening was not made any better by Samaranch's line that the Games had been "exceptional," after he had called all the previous ones "the best ever." This included Lillehammer, where he had been publicly called a fascist and where the Norwegian athlete had at first refused to take the oath on behalf of all Olympians because of Samaranch. The IOC president had threatened to go back to Lausanne because of the brouhaha. Yet, somehow those Games were "the best ever." Clearly, he was saying ours weren't. It was as if he had poked the entire city in the eye. President Clinton evened the score a few days later when, with the U.S. Olympians in attendance at the White House, he called the Atlanta Games, "the best Games ever," but it was small consolation to the committee.

I am often asked why he chose to give us a lukewarm pat on the back. I don't know, but can only surmise that the city's lack of support which resulted in the trashy look and snarled traffic in the downtown, plus the technology glitches helped him come to that conclusion. I have another theory as well. I think the bombing brought back bad memories of Munich, which the IOC had tried over the years to sweep under the carpet. Take all of the above and you have the ingredients for a bad-tasting stew.

Billy was very philosophical about the whole thing but A. D. was livid. He took Samaranch's comments as a personal insult and was ready to do battle in our last press conference, but Billy prevailed and our meeting with the media was uneventful. I think Charlie Battle, Linda Stephenson, and Ginger Watkins felt slightly betrayed by the IOC's attitude. After giving almost ten years of their lives to the effort, they deserved better. Fortunately, columnist Colin Campbell came riding to the rescue. The whole thing was my fault. It was a relief to us all to have his expert opinion on the subject.

Melissa Turner, who three-and-a-half years earlier, had lauded me a "flaming torch," decided the press couldn't get their information on time and their buses to go where they wanted them to go because I was "arrogant." I was blamed for everything from routing the torch around Greenville County (partly guilty) to insulating ACOG from the media (not guilty). She had me sounding like Rasputin on uppers. I wasn't upset. Being called arrogant by the *Atlanta Journal-Constitution* is akin to being called ugly by a wart hog.

The best part of Turner's attack on me was that the day the story came out, I was at my childhood church to celebrate its 150th anniversary. I saw a lot of people I hadn't seen since my mother had died a few years earlier. One dear old lady came up and told me she had seen the article in the paper about me that day. Before I could explain what was behind the story, she took my hand and patted it and said, "I'm just sorry your Mama wasn't alive to read it. She would have been so proud." So much for the power of the press.

How do you define whether the Games were good or not? Not by the media's thumb-sucking. Billy Payne had put it in perspective. The media's frustrations with their own transportation problems and their own technology problems would be perceived by the world as the media's problems. They certainly wouldn't define the 1996 Games. And they didn't.

First, look at the numbers. Start with the ones that count. We had more athletes participate than ever, around 10,000. They managed to set thirty-two world records and 111 Olympic records. We sold 8.6 million tickets, an all-time record and more than Barcelona and Los Angeles combined and had more than five million spectators in attendance. Some 209 million people saw NBC's superb coverage, making it the most-watched event in television history at the time. More than 5.5 million people had passed through Centennial Park in the twenty days of its operation. They saw more than 400,000 personalized bricks that people had purchased to commemorate the Centennial Games. Most importantly, we had raised $1.7 billion privately and had constructed some $500 million in permanent facilities and left no public debt.

Our Cultural Olympiad had been an enormous success on its own. More than a quarter of a million tickets were sold to the various performances and exhibitions. Under the direction of Linda Stephenson and Dr. Jeffrey Babcock, we had gathered most of the world's living Nobel Laureates in Literature. The "Rings: Five Passions in World Art" was an extraordinary art exhibit that was ten times larger than any exhibition ever presented at Atlanta's High Museum and featured works of Rodin, Picasso, and Matisse, as well as works from unknown artists from ancient times. More than 200,000 saw the show. There were performances by Georgia native Jessye Norman, Wynton Marsalis, the London Chamber Orchestra, the Russian National Orchestra, the Australian Youth Orchestra, and the Royal Thai Ballet. The Southern Crossroads Festival, featuring the song and dance of our region, attracted more than 100,000 people a day with 1,000 different performances from noon to past midnight.

We had involved almost every school in the state in our "Olympic Day in the Schools" program to help increase students awareness in the Olympic ideals. We operated an International Youth Camp during the Games for some 500 kids from 155 countries.

We had created the Olympic Force made up of some 1800 organizations and 7500 people from around the state that over four years collected some seventy-five tons of food and a tractor-trailer of new toys, more than a quarter of a million children's books for the state's libraries.

174

More than 10,000 volunteers worked in state and community parks planting trees and removing trash.

There was so much for which to be proud. Baron Pierre de Courbertin, founder of the modern Olympic movement once said, "The important thing in the Olympic Games is not winning, but taking part, for the essential thing in life is not conquering but fighting well."

There were 100,000 people who helped put on the 1996 Centennial Olympic Games. They had fought well and left with heads held high.

# 12

## AFTERMATH

Since the Atlanta Games ended in August 1996, the Olympic movement
has fallen on hard times. It was bound to happen. The Olympic Games
had gotten too big, too rich, too arrogant, and too insular. Cities were
falling all over themselves for the privilege of hosting the Games; not
because they wanted an opportunity to bring people together in a
peaceful celebration, but rather for the financial windfall sure to come as
a result. Instead of Olympic rings, everybody sees dollar signs: The
chambers of commerce, local businesses, special interest groups, media
advertising departments. To rephrase John Kennedy, "Ask not what you
can do for the Games; ask what the Games can do for you." This is what
makes Billy Payne unique. He went after the 1996 Olympic Games for
the right reasons. He saw an inherent goodness of the Olympic
movement that was overlooked by most everybody else.

Clearly, the International Olympic Committee lost its bearings. The
movement was almost bankrupt in 1984. Just look at what had preceded
Los Angeles. There was the terrorism in Munich in 1972. The financial
disaster in Montreal in 1976. President Carter had refused to allow the
United States to compete in Moscow in 1980 because of the Soviet
Union's invasion of Afghanistan, and the Soviets reciprocated by
boycotting the Games in 1984. The Olympic Games were damaged
goods. Peter Ueberroth rescued the Games by showing the IOC how the
Olympics could be corporately financed and then proceeded to stage
enormously successful Games. He did them no favors with his lessons.

With the Los Angeles experience behind them, the International
Olympic Committee became convinced of its own invincibility. I have
spent a lot of my career in the external environment, dealing with self-
righteous politicians and self-important media snobs, but as a whole, the

IOC ranks among the most supercilious crowd I have ever been around. Had I been a part of the bid committee, I might have felt differently toward them, but having come out of the pragmatic environment of big business, I found the group terribly pompous. The members deem themselves royalty—some are—and conduct themselves as such. Few I got to know well. Most of them neither knew who I was nor cared. I was just another faceless worker ant. There were some exceptions. Perhaps the nicest of all was Prince Albert of Monaco. He probably had the most reason to be affected by the pomp and circumstance within the IOC, but clearly wasn't. Pal Schmitt of Hungary was another member who was friendly and professional. Kevin Gosper, chairman of the press commission who has taken his lumps in his native Australia since the Games were award to Sydney, was courteous and businesslike in his dealings. Even Dick Pound, the chairman of our coordination commission, was friendly.

As for the IOC in general, I have described them as the College of Cardinals, populated by a hundred Machiavellis. Mix high-powered people from all over the world in an organization with power, money, and influence and you have the International Olympic Committee.

It reminds me of a joke that is told on the religious denomination of your choice. A group was touring heaven with an angel as their guide. As they passed groups sitting on clouds, the angel would announce what denomination they had just seen. As the tour went by one particularly surly looking group, one of the visitors asked, "Who are they?" "Shh," the angel admonished. "Don't let them see us. They think they are the only ones here."

I found that an apt description of many of the IOC members. The late Primo Nibiolo once refused to get out of his limousine until a red carpet had been rolled out for him. I witnessed Francois Carrard, director-general of the IOC, berate a helpless volunteer at Lillehammer because his car was not out front when he came downstairs. The wife of one IOC member complained because there were not fresh flowers in the ladies room at Sanford Stadium during the Olympic soccer matches. Members were aghast at the protocol breach committed by President Clinton during the Games when he invited the winning members of the U.S. women's gymnastic team to visit him and the First Lady while seated in the VIP section, reserved only for IOC members. No one was allowed in their special section, especially athletes.

This kind of thinking carried over to the way cities were expected to bid on the Games. It is fair to say that the International Olympic Committee was rather loose in the interpretation and enforcement of the rules. Their main rule was if you wanted the Games in your city, then show us. Wine and dine us. Entertain us. Give us little favors. As former U.S. Attorney General Griffin Bell told Congress, the whole process "encouraged a practice of lobbying IOC members in which excess was inherent." With a number of cities salivating to be selected to host the Olympic Games (remember the financial windfall), it was a disaster waiting to happen. And, finally, it did.

After Marc Hodler, an IOC member from Switzerland, went public with complaints on Salt Lake City's bid efforts in late 1998, the Olympic house didn't completely cave in but it sagged severely. The host city for the 2002 Games was accused of payoffs and special treatment for members of the International Olympic Committee and their families, including questionable travel, scholarships and even jobs. There were charges of vote buying and influence peddling. At first, there was denial by the IOC. But as the facts began to emerge it became obvious there had been abuses of the bidding process. As a result, ten members of the IOC were either expelled or resigned and the bids of Atlanta, Toronto, and Sydney were put under the microscope. It is here that the press gets another black eye. For members of the Olympic press commission, which includes the largest media organizations in the world, to say they were unaware of the alleged practices, is naïve at best and dishonest at worst.

Cover me with sour grapes, but I would suggest that had the press spent more time watching and reporting on the long-time "inherent excess" of the host city bidding process and less time complaining about their creature comforts, they would have had the story long before Mr. Hodler handed it to them on a silver platter. In fact, they were as imperious as the IOC members themselves. Being oblivious to what was going on under their noses just doesn't wash. They were too chummy with the people they were supposed to cover.

Even the *Atlanta Journal-Constitution* deserves a rap on the knuckles. When the storm broke over the Olympic scandals, they sprung into action, demanding that all bid information be made available to them immediately so that they could investigate whether there were improprieties in the bid efforts of the Atlanta Organizing Committee. Had I been the editor, I think I would have asked the staff where the hell they were when the bid effort was taking place and how could it have been conducted and them not know what was going on. I wasn't remotely involved in the bid and I knew of the gifts and first class travel given to the IOC members and their families. Evidently, everybody in town seemed to know but the newspaper, because a lot of people were involved beside the ten original volunteers, working hard on the Atlanta bid and you're damn sure not going to win by telling one of the Olympic poobahs, "If you happen to be coming to Atlanta sometime, why don't you drop by and let us tell you about the city's worthiness to host the Games. You *are* a member of the IOC, aren't you?" If it took a first class airplane trip and a limousine ride and a piece of crystal, so be it. To the business mavens in town, that was a small price to pay for the resultant glory of hosting the Games. And the newspaper didn't know this? Yeah, right.

Colin Campbell, who in my opinion, can say less in more words that anybody I've ever known—including me—led the charge. Dull on a good day, he had gotten downright tedious since the demise of Izzy, and ACOG's refusal to give up the information he wanted when he wanted gave his life new purpose. It was the committee's position that the organization was private and not subject to the open records laws of Georgia. But it was a stance not worth the fight and the records were made public. Alas, Campbell couldn't find a smoking gun, and as a matter of fact, couldn't find anything that would guarantee him the column inches necessary to soldier on.

Recently, an independent ethics panel appointed by the IOC and free from their influence reported that the "sins" of the Atlanta committee were so "trivial" they did not warrant further investigation. This was the same thing that former Griffin Bell had said in his report to Congress. Hopefully, this positive report got the intrepid newshounds off the hook with their bosses for a serious case of sloppy reporting during the bid effort in Atlanta. Perhaps now the *Atlanta Journal-Constitution* can get back to other issues, like the racial divide in Atlanta—a less easy target than ACOG.

He hasn't said so publicly or privately, but I think the whole episode has hurt and bewildered Billy Payne. I have told him—and I believe this with all my heart—when the history of Atlanta is written in years to come, he will be judged a hero and his detractors won't even rate a footnote. It has been heartening to hear the reaction of the rank-and-file citizens of Atlanta. The public has better judgment than we give them credit for and all of the publicity since the Games hasn't changed their strong positive feelings for Billy.

And, thankfully, none of the scandal of the past few years will in any way hurt the movement, because what the ancient Greeks discovered many centuries ago works today and will work tomorrow. The Olympic Games are about getting people together and having them striving to do their best against the best in peaceful competition. In our sophisticated, high-tech society we haven't come up with better suggestions than the Olympic ideal.

Billy Payne made a believer out of me. There is an inherent goodness about the Olympic movement that money, power, and influence can't dilute. Neither can out-of-touch old aristocrats who think that because of their status in the IOC, they are the Olympic Games. The marketing deals, the television contracts, the special interest groups who want a piece of the action, the economic development moguls, petty politicians, squabbling neighborhoods—none of these can weaken the concept.

The Olympic Games are for the athletes. That is what has saved the Olympic movement from itself. It isn't just for the high-profile stars from powerful countries but for the kayaker who had to put duct tape on his vessel to keep it from sinking while he practiced. Or for the woman who had to train at night so that she wouldn't be a tempting target for snipers. Or the young people from all over the world who came to Georgia to practice and got to know local citizens and at the same time introduced the locals to their own cultures. People who would never have known the other existed without the Centennial Games. It is a 99-pound janitor from South Africa winning the Olympic men's marathon and an Ethiopian farmer's daughter taking the gold medal in the women's marathon. It is Kerry Strug nailing a perfect vault on a badly strained ankle. It is Fred Alderman and George Beard watching four young men outrun everybody else in the 4x400 meter relay as they had sixty-eight years earlier.

Everybody who showed up in Atlanta to compete was a champion. No matter what happens to them in the future, they can all say that for at least one day in 1996, they were an Olympian. That is what makes the Olympic Games worth the effort.

It is also important to note that while two million people showed up to watch the Games, there were no riots, no fights, no shootings—just strangers celebrating with strangers. Atlanta's streets may have been trashy, but for once they were safe. One deranged soul planted a bomb but, despite the tragedy, succeeded only in bringing us all closer together.

Bud Greenspan, the great cinematographer of the modern Olympic Games and a good friend, tells the story of John Stephen Akhwari of Tanzania, the last runner in the Mexico City marathon in 1968. Akhwari was an hour behind everyone else. His leg was bloodied and bandaged but he was determined to hobble around the track to the finish line as the crowd roared its appreciation at his courage. Afterwards, asked why he didn't quit since he was going to finish last anyway, Ahkwari gave this memorable answer, "My country did not send me to Mexico City to start the race. They sent me to finish the race."

There will continue to be controversies in the Olympic movement. I suspect that there were even some squabbles before the athletes showed up in Olympia 2700 years ago and they are still going on. Look no further than Sydney and Salt Lake City and Athens, home of the 2004 Games. There will continue to be disputes over where to build venues, who will build them and how they will be paid for and who will be in charge. The cities that don't win the host city bid will continue to cry "foul." There will be fights over tickets, television contracts, and sponsorship deals. I am not naïve enough to think that the long-needed reform movement in the IOC is going to make the allure of the cash register disappear.

But in spite of all of that, there will also be a John Stephen Akhwari determined to make it to the finish line because that is what he was sent there to do. He won't win a gold medal but he will be able to say he had done his best because somebody gave him the opportunity. As long as that is that is the case, it will be worth the effort.

There were a lot of days when I didn't believe that. Today, I do.

Thank you, Billy.

# Epilogue

In June 1998, I received a call from the editor of the *Atlanta Business Chronicle* to do a retrospective on Atlanta two years after the Games. The paper's publisher, Ed Baker, was astounded at the little attention given to the impact of the Olympic Games on the city of Atlanta by the press and had suggested I do a guest column. I eagerly accepted.

I'm not sure what the paper was expecting, but as I have so stated in this book, I said Atlanta blew a great opportunity and proceeded to state my reasons. Having turned in the column, I left with my wife, my son Ken, and daughter-in-law Jackie for a long-awaited trip to Scotland. Being retired, I no longer felt compelled to check phone messages, as I had had to do in my earlier Type-A lifestyle. I waited a week or so and decided to see if anyone had called. I was astounded. My voice mailbox was overflowing with calls from people, praising my courage to say what needed to be said about the city. I had touched a nerve and I can't say that it was preordained. I had said what I felt, not knowing that so many people would agree.

The reaction was not good news to Jane. After suffering through thirty-five years of my high-profile jobs, she thought she had me tamed and ready for a life of flower gardens and antiquing. When I returned to Atlanta, Ed Baker asked me to consider a regular column in the *Business Chronicle*. I accepted.

For the next year-and-a-half, I said all the things I have always wanted to say but couldn't in the corporate world. I joke in my speeches today that I have traded three-syllable corporate jargon for one-syllable terms and I leave little doubt how I feel on a variety of subjects. I have a lot of topics from which to choose—business, politics, education, the news media, even the public relations business. You name it and I have probably written about it and angered someone in the process. I have skewered Atlanta City Hall and earned their enmity in doing so. It got so bad at one point that I quit writing because of Jane's distress at seeing me constantly branded a "racist" by Mayor Bill Campbell's henchmen. Then I decided that I should consider the source. If I let them win because I couldn't take the heat, shame on me. Also, I remember the public relations axiom—never pick a fight with those who buy their ink by the barrel, something they haven't yet discovered.

I have since had the opportunity to expand my pontifications statewide and am in the process of doing so today. But I would never have gotten to this point in my new life without my buddy Ed Baker's encouragement.

When the opportunity to do this book came my way, it was hard going back and reading the daily entries that I recorded as I drove to and from work. At the time I was making the tapes, I had no idea how the whole thing would come out and I now listen to myself being angry with me and others. Frequently, I expressed a lot of doubt as to why I had retired from BellSouth and had subjected my family to all the stress and I wondered why everybody couldn't see what Billy Payne saw. Would I regret, I asked myself on tape, having made the effort? It was my wise physician, Harry Cheves, who supplied the answer. "The mind is a wonderful thing," the good doctor said, "As the years pass, it will allow you to remember the good things and it will block out the bad times." As usual, he was right. There were some very good times in all of the stress that are getting better as the years pass.

This book has helped me let go of the frustrations I hear on my tapes. I have said all I need to say on the subject. I will leave it to you to form your own opinions of us, knowing that I have only scratched the surface of that complex effort and the people who were a part of it. I strove for absolute accuracy in the facts but chances are that I may have gotten a number wrong. If so, forgive me.

I doubt that what I have said on these pages will be warmly embraced by the power structure in Atlanta and maybe even by some of my colleagues at the Atlanta Committee for the Olympic Games, who have their own perspective on the Centennial Games, but I stand by my opinions and will be happy to debate any issue with anyone who disagrees with my views. My disappointment in Atlanta's performance doesn't extend to its people. Atlantans showed that Southern Hospitality is alive and very well as did the people of the state of Georgia. In the end, that is how we will be remembered.

I am blessed with a patient and understanding wife, two terrific kids who found equally wonderful spouses, and in turn, gave me four grandsons. It was these four boys who showed me what was really important in life—and it is not living in the past. It is time to finally say goodbye to 1996 and to spend what years I have left enjoying a family I don't deserve.

But, just to be on the safe side, I am buying one more barrel of ink.

# INDEX

BRODART, CO.  Cat. No. 23-221-003

## DATE DUE